S0-AAA-192

LIFE: THE WHOLE ENCHILADA

LIFE: THE WH●LE ENCHILADA

A GRATITUDE MEMOIR

JOHN R. O'NEIL

Red Pepper Moon Press

Sausalito, California

Copyright 2020 by John R. O'Neil

All Rights Reserved

No part of this book may be reproduced in any form or by any electronic or mechanical
means, including information storage or retrieval systems, without permission in writing
from the publisher, except by a reviewer, who may quote brief passages in a review.

Cover design by Grace Vannelli.

For more information about the ideas in this book,
please visit: www.redpeppermoon.com

ISBN 978-1-09834-319-4 (pbk) | ISBN 978-1-09834-320-0 (ebook)

A highly personal book like this one needs someone with many talents and lots of verve to support the jittery writer.

Pat, my wise and funny wife is made for this role.

My gratitude knows no bounds.

Contents

PROLOGUE

...

Words are our first tools. Words soon become questions, the vehicles of curiosity. As a child, my questions and curiosity were boundless. I was drawn to anyone who would patiently listen to my words and answer my questions, satisfy (for the moment) my curiosity, and stoke my excitement. Now in what I consider my "Bonus Years," I'm writing this book, in part, to give faces to people in my life who showed up rather magically to share in my curiosity, excitement, and often fervor about certain questions.

I was blessed to have rich, early sources of words: books and adult talk. My parents were rarely without a book, and dinner was usually an occasion for lively, even heated, discussions. Guests were often invited because they had something special to discuss. Both my parents worked, and their wonderful love and wisdom were complemented by two caregivers and teachers: Swate, my nature guide, and his partner Matty, cooking maven. Both were masterful curiosity connoisseurs.

Swate and Matty, Curiosity Connoisseurs

Swate managed our gardens and helped keep our family's Southern California ranch functioning. He arrived during the dust bowl exodus in 1938 with his partner Matty, a roundish commander of the kitchen. They were African Americans from Louisiana and Texas. They ran things and watched over me, a skinny, blonde, eager seven-year-old.

Every minute that I wasn't in school, I dogged Swate and asked questions as he went about his work. He was astonishingly patient and loved nature. Tall and strong, Swate rarely found a task he couldn't do: Fix the irrigation system—check. Plant the right thing in the right place to thrive in the hot, dry desert near Palm Springs—check. Help build submarine buildings—check. And so on.

Swate was a keen observer of nature, a generous storyteller, and he loved to sing and laugh (often at my antics and ignorance). "Where do stink bugs get their smell?" I asked. Smiling widely, Swate answered, "They get awful stomach aches from eating stink weed and skunk cabbage."

Swate told me a story of how to deal with rattlesnakes. "You get them stretched out so they can't coil up and strike, you grab them by the tail and spin them around, and then you snap them like a whip." Later, my father said he admired Swate's creativity, but added, "Better leave that method to the specialists and just avoid rattlers."

Perhaps my parents favorite exchange between me and Swate was this one: "Swate," I asked, "How did you get so strong and can I do it, too?" Swate, after looking me up and down, replied, "When I was a boy, we had a calf that I watched over from when it was first born. I used to lift that calf over my head every day, as it got bigger and bigger, until I could lift a cow." Having no calf, I wondered what to do and Swate had an answer, "We will put rocks in that bucket. Every day you can lift it, and every day we will add more rocks."

I started immediately, to my parents' astonishment and delight. I can only imagine the laughs they enjoyed, seeing me walk around the garden with a bucket full of rocks held aloft.

At established times, Matty allowed me in her kitchen for a treat. Her goal was to "add some meat to my bones." She would allow me to sit on a stool and watch her make certain dishes, like gumbo, my father's favorite. To fresh okra, garlic, and tomatoes from Swate's garden, she added chicken and lots of spices. I learned the joy of food chemistry, Matty style. She told me how much and in what order she used each ingredient that went into this magical gift from New Orleans.

When I found Matty's cooking too peppery for my young taste buds (but perfect for my father's) she suggested building my tolerance.

Each day, I would get hotter and hotter food until eventually I could eat hot peppers. Sound familiar? It's another version of calf-lifting.

|||||||||||||||||||||||||||||||||||||||||||||||||||||||||||||||||||||||||||||||||||||||||||||||||||||||||||||||||||||||||||||||||||||||||||||||||||||||||||||||||||||||

WHAT TO LEARN:

Magic is everywhere for the asking and miracles abound, especially in nature. Keep looking, asking, and honoring everyone who teaches you.

|||||||||||||||||||||||||||||||||||||||||||||||||||||||||||||||||||||||||||||||||||||||||||||||||||||||||||||||||||||||||||||||||||||||||||||||||||||||||||||||||||||||

Carrying Curiosity Forward: My Circuitous Learning Journey

I am what I learn. Day by day and year by year I stay alive by discovering curiosity-driven questions and by evolving through lessons on character shaping. When this goes well, life is indeed a feast filled with delicious satisfactions and delightful characters. When life becomes repetitive and boring, I am literally starving—emotionally, intellectually, and socially. My prospects go from caviar to gruel.

Looking back, I realize that I've always been seduced by shiny new learning challenges. I believe you can arrange to continually find sources of intellectual and spiritual disruption throughout life—if you're willing to risk entering each new epoch by throwing out old, comfortable theories and tired assumptions. I adhered to this approach, which is why my entire life has been made up of a series of mini-careers. Luckily, lots of good people nudged me along, altering my smug trajectories. The following outline of my journey from youth to today demonstrates how disruptions in my thinking led to learning, growth, and transformation:

- One of my high school teachers rattled my cage by insisting I could and should write prose and poetry.

- As a US Air Force training instructor, I taught pilots to survive in Korea. At the same time, the Great Books Seminars prodded me to read Russian classics by Dostoevsky, Chekhov, and Tolstoy. While these were dangerous books to be checking out of a military base library during the McCarthy Era, with its fear of the "Red Menace," they were most helpful in exploring how life is actually lived.

- Rushing to complete my undergraduate degree in record time, I discovered three UC Berkeley professors who each challenged and altered my academic future, including then-chancellor Clark Kerr who risked allowing me to take his graduate seminar as an undergraduate.

- While working on large switched networks like SABER, the airline reservation system, as well as other more exotic tasks at AT&T in New York City, my limo driver warned that I was becoming boring. He was right. In spite of perks and title, I was boring—and bored.

- Having returned to California, I simultaneously undertook two new learning curves: Investing, with two partners, in early-stage companies in Silicon Valley, and studying Jungian psychology. I rapidly learned that the combination was too far a reach. I got out of the investing business fairly quickly, supporting my partners in their efforts instead.

- After attending graduate school while going through psychoanalysis, I dove right into the chilly waters of higher education, serving as vice president of Mills College. I eventually became president of a four-campus graduate school of psychology with 2,500 students.

- I've written and hustled three books on leadership and gratitude. My first book, *The Paradox of Success: When Winning at Work Means Losing at Life*[1], tossed me into the frothy world of Davos, which led to for-hire speaking, consulting, board service, and advising leaders engaged in dynamic changes in their lives and careers.

- Together with other learning questers including my talented friend, Pete Thigpen, I fashioned an Aspen Institute-like program called "The Good Life Seminar," and led long-weekend events limited to 20 people at Cavallo Point in Sausalito and select venues in England.

- Ever haunted by my prophetic high school teacher, I now find I've come full circle, working on yet another slippery-slope writing project (this one), for which I took up the craft of composing ("whitish") hip-hop poetry.

This is not the book I set out to write. I originally started an updated and expanded book on life-stage development: What we are supposed to learn at each life stage and how to go about it. However, once I started, the questions of **how** we learn and **who** guides us became the central and important questions. In *Seasons of Grace*[2], an earlier book that I co-authored with partner Alan Jones, then Dean of Grace Cathedral in San Francisco, we explored the healing that expressing gratitude can bring to us. In writing this memoir, I returned to ask, "Who helps us and guides us with the learning that we need in each life stage?" I then began to identify many of the important teachers, mentors, and character shapers who showed up in my own life, and I discovered and wrote about the deep gratitude I feel for each one. Thus, the subtitle shifted from "A Learning Memoir" to "A Gratitude Memoir."

A work of this kind should **not** be seen as science, with its tough-minded approach to the type of experimentation that strives for repeatable results. As William James said of the study of psychology,

"I wished, by treating Psychology like a natural science, to help her to become one."[3]

The ancient Greeks had it right by presenting life lessons as theater, wherein the audience was actively involved. Theater has a heritage of helping audiences heal through both intellectual and visceral learning. Poets, psychologists, playwrights, and philosophers have helped fill in gaps in our learning lives. For example, Freud conceived the Oedipus complex from the Greek drama, *Oedipus Rex* by Sophocles.

Here are some philosophical observations that have guided me in shaping the direction of this book:

- "If you do not tell the truth about yourself you cannot tell it about other people."—Virginia Woolf[4]

- "All the world's a stage,/ And all the men and women merely players:/ They have their exits and their entrances;/ And one man in his time plays many parts,/ His acts being seven ages."—William Shakespeare[5]

- "Explanations exist; they have existed for all time; there is always a well-known solution to every human problem—neat, plausible, and wrong."—H.L. Mencken[6]

- "Nothing is so firmly believed as that which we least know."—Michel de Montaigne[7]

- "Human history becomes more and more a race between education and catastrophe."—H.G. Wells[8]

Adult Development, Leadership, and Learning

One of my teachers and intellectual heroes was Abraham Maslow, author of *Motivation and Personality*[9] and a pioneering developmental psychologist. Maslow's well-known "Hierarchy of Human Needs" posits a brilliant model of adult development. At the bottom are the various basic human needs such as food and shelter; at the top is something termed "self-actualization," or the work of growing intellectually and spiritually as a person.

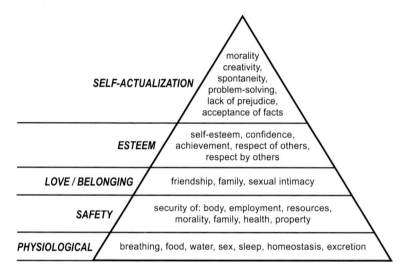

Maslow's Hierarchy of Human Needs

Abe, a funny, smart, down-home person, was fascinated by the leaders at the top tier—the most self-actualized—who might be called "the learning elite." These are the people who work hard at knowing themselves and growing their basic characters—their rootstocks. When writing my book, *The Paradox of Success*, I luckily found some of Abe's winners, and from their stories I went about extracting and recording what attitudes and actions make good learners over all aspects of life. The reader will have the pleasure of discovering who arrived when these students came up with the right questions to prove their learning readiness. I studied with many of these people, and they supported me in my own struggle for maturation.

WHAT TO LEARN:

I love the image of the Zen master who keeps pouring tea into a student's full cup. When the startled student brings the spillage to the master's attention, he replies, "The cup is like your mind—too full to learn." Point made. I try to keep my cup empty, as often as possible.

The core problem that sapiens face is ignorance about the consequences of their own behavior and its effect on evolution. Life has been trial and error, with each tribe adopting their own belief system. Then, in their rapturous expression of these beliefs, they decide to impose them on others whose belief systems differ. Wars are fought to sort it out and little true learning ensues. This pattern is repeated again and again. In the process, the planet we live on becomes damaged and weary.

I see us as careening through life as if we were balls in a pinball machine, pulled by gravity while being whacked by paddles and distracted by pinging noises and flashing lights. Hopes, fears, and needs shift from one life act to another. Each family, tribe, and nation make differing demands on us, as we try to achieve culturally defined success. A Haitian family living in the Bronx extracts different developmental demands from their children than those of a tribal village in Botswana. But one common commandment might be: **Learn yourself forward.** I examine the efficacy of that approach in the coming pages.

As I live out my life, I often recall a line from the Broadway hit, Auntie Mame, "Life is a banquet and most poor suckers are starving to death."[10] Curiosity plays a critical role in finding others to join the banquet of learning delights.

This book is an attempt to help readers set their own banquet tables, with all the trimmings—and I urge each reader to write their own small book as a legacy. One early reader, Becky Mayer, said, "I read awhile, stop, write a bit, think, and then go back to reading." This is a book to sip, not gulp.

SETTING THE STAGE

...

"All the world's a stage,
And all the men and women mere players:
They have their exits and their entrances;
And one man in his time plays many parts."

— Jaques in *As You Like It* by **William Shakespeare**

Life journeys are really quests, through which we seek life's answers. And roles change in each of life's acts. Often roles are clownish. Perhaps that's when humans are at their best. The mythologist Joseph Campbell called quests "hero journeys."[11] He found them in every culture. They have common elements: discovery, victories and defeats, visions, virtues, and general life lessons. But never did Campbell find or recognize humor in these journeys, and I find that sad. As I write this memoir of my own life journey, and perhaps as you record your own, I hope we can enjoy the odd chuckle as we notice our humanness.

The Players

It's abundantly clear that we need guides to help us learn. We require dramatic personae to help solve the thematic inquiry of each life act and, of course, the players must change for the next act. For each act of life's drama, I set learning goals that I trust will attract new partners, guides, and teachers. Armed with well-considered and energizing questions, we can pursue the guides we need. Guides appear to be of three basic types:

- **Teachers and Mentors** offer hidden treasures and arcane practices involved in learning and growing.

- **Character Shapers** come in many different forms, starting with my family.

- **Wisdom Carriers** are often authors or playwrights. For some of us, poets and artists bring wisdom and inspiration. For lucky people like me, friends and working partners bring a flow of insights and a zeal to learn.

These guides bring us knowledge from their own life experiences. I have uncovered my own guides through mutual curiosity expressed. One big change in my life that brought significant and ongoing guidance came when I had just been discharged from the Air Force and was entering UC Berkeley. I was literally tap dancing with excitement and curiosity. Various characters showed up, starting with my statistics professor who asked me to be his teaching assistant, then sponsored me for an unusual assignment: A certain Dr. Rogers from Harvard was conducting a special summer seminar to design the controls for an automated refinery. He asked if I would like to join this highly diverse design team. The answer was, "Yes." That exposure caught the attention of Marv Epstein, a lead computer scientist on the AT&T recruiting team with whom I would later work on another fascinating assignment. Marv and I became life-long friends.

Now in my bonus years, I am delighted to have teachers and mentors who have become my learning partners. We generally share common interests and passions for topics like writing (especially poetry), politics, and leadership. There are many ways for learning quests to proceed. Many guides and advisors may show up along the way, and we can use a taxonomy that describes the various types to help recruit the right people.

Great Teachers and Mentors

Mentors teach, but they often have an experience edge over teachers. Both instill and reinforce our natural curiosity, yet they come in varying styles and forms. My fifth-grade teacher, Miss Voss, was a tall, imposing woman with gray and brown hair who always wore practical shoes. Her passion for birds and animals was contagious. So, thanks to Miss Voss, on a trip to Patagonia decades later, I found myself enrolling in nature walks featuring birds and animals.

Mentors are magical. Take Merlin, King Arthur's mentor, who transformed nature to keep young Arthur enthralled with learning and, moreover, humble. None of my mentors were magicians, but they did help me reconsider tired and overused assumptions.

The term "mentor' derives from Homer's epic *Odyssey*, in which King Odysseus entrusts the education of his son Telemachus to his old friend, Mentor, when he leaves for the Trojan War.[12] Many wealthy families of ancient Greece sought out philosophers like Socrates and his student Plato as tutors, and in turn, King Philip of Macedonia hired Plato's student Aristotle to instruct his son Alexander. The tradition of mentoring still carries on today.

Teachers and mentors are typically older life veterans, but they may also be younger. Keep an eye out the youthful guide with special knowledge and a belly full of fire.

Character Shapers

In every aspect of every life act, I have sought Character Shapers. Some have arrived through stories or drama, while others have lived down the street. Heroic figures like Eleanor Roosevelt and Nelson Mandela have offered demonstrations of character in how they lived and led. I was drawn to their stories and instructed by their actions.

Theater and literature offer audiences and readers many stories of moral development. *The Merchant of Venice*, Shakespeare's tragedy about a money lender and his struggles, teaches us about tolerance. In *To Kill a Mockingbird*, Harper Lee's tale of a black man rescued from a false accusation in a small Southern town in the 1930s, we learn about justice and compassion along with the young narrator Scout, from her father, lawyer Atticus Finch.[13]

Athletes and coaches may play the role of Character Shapers, and many try. Lad Burgin, a friend and colleague who played American college football under controversial Ohio State coach Woody Hayes, has carried his wisdom on leadership and character shaping into corporate board rooms. So has legendary UCLA basketball coach, John Wooden.

The people who played the role of Character Shapers in my life (and some who still do) arrived when I was untethered, searching, and ready to learn. The process of discovery may be deliberate, or it might be synchronistic, but being ripe and open is needed for magic to occur.

Wisdom Carriers

In every culture, there are those who carry and spread wisdom. In his short book *Civilization on Trial*, Arnold Toynbee describes people he calls "culture carriers."[14] These are the poets, artists, and philosophers who highlight the "saving remnants" of a dying civilization. For many of us, it was a timely book that posed mind-boggling questions and helped us consider our unexamined assumptions.

Every time I hear a symphony or read a new poem, I am grateful to Wisdom Carrier Rollo Jones, a teacher who made great music and good writing part of the everyday lives of high school boys. He made "high culture" available and enjoyable to us. J.D. Salinger did the trick for many in my generation, with his book, *The Catcher in the Rye*.[15]

A Note about Special Guides

A big challenge in writing this book was presenting the guides in my own life who kept me moving forward—people who, in their wisdom, would also inspire readers. This meant having to leave out many dear friends and precious children, who most certainly helped shape my development. And the hardest person to position was my wife Pat, who plays many roles in my life, ranging from muse to Eros. As I write this in the high desert of Oregon, we're celebrating our 30th wedding anniversary. Here is a brief story on how we got this far: When we bumped into each other on a lovely day on Union Street in San Francisco, we had known each other for years, but we had drifted apart and our marriages were behind us. We were, as they say, "good friends," but now we were free to be more, much more. We're still "catching up," having fun, and supporting each other in a hard-core romp of a marriage. Not a day goes by without our sharing loving thoughts as we relish each other's company, and the mutual learning journey we enjoy.

||||||||||||||||||||||||||||||||||||||||||||||||||||||||||||||||||||||||||||||||||||||||||||||||||||||||||||||||||||||||||||||||||||||||||||||||||||||||||

WHAT TO LEARN:

Fresh guides are always needed to enhance intellectual and spiritual practices. The big quandary for readers might be how their curiosity can be fed. Where are the Mentors, Teachers, Character Shapers, and Wisdom Carriers for the next stage of life? Finding the right people becomes a challenge. It's tempting to say, "The lessons will come along when I am primed, especially with the ripe queries I encounter during career and job changes." Perhaps they will magically surface, but it usually takes focused effort on the learner's part.

||||||||||||||||||||||||||||||||||||||||||||||||||||||||||||||||||||||||||||||||||||||||||||||||||||||||||||||||||||||||||||||||||||||||||||||||||||||||||

Plot Development

At each stage of human development, curiosity must be regained by shifting to new frontiers: Puzzles must be more challenging; learning partners and teams must replace solo ventures; plain and concrete must give way to complex and abstract; knowledge gathering must evolve into wisdom creation.

The most fortunate students find teachers who morph into learning partners. My learning partners have often been my friends and business associates, as well as clients seeking to expand their capabilities and develop their core strengths. My clients offer a special opportunity for mutual learning that involves metrics: I help them set measurable goals. I also provide them with information on friends and leaders who trace their successes to being focused on learning.

Making Curiosity a Profit Driver

My current work is to serve leaders who are facing challenges and growing, by helping them develop learning organizations. In a world under constant assault from ignorance, the best leaders are working on ways to solve the most difficult questions. That involves creating an environment where learning and curiosity are prized and supported. There is great leverage in this mission.

Fortunately for me, I have two wonderful learning partners. One of them is Yury Boshyk, who founded and runs the Global Learning Network. Their annual gatherings draw as many as 2,000 attendees, mostly Chief Learning Officers (CLOs). Yury has fostered a climate of trust and sharing, allowing the members to test fresh ideas on one another. The other is Margaret Downs, a leadership maven, consultant, and coach. She and her husband Henry are friends and fellow seekers of "the good life."

As Yury pointed out during a seminar we led together, "We are discovering how much the subject of learning is becoming the cornerstone of corporate growth and development. The challenges facing Chief Learning Officers are that both problem complexity and methods of learning are shifting daily. Advanced digital techniques using various media and artificial intelligence must match the speed of emerging fresh quandaries, dilemmas, and global competition."

Uncovering the Right Questions

As different problems are pursued and the content shifts, fresh thinking is needed, so a big part of our learning future must be with partners, triads, and teams. Such teams relish questions that stretch them collectively and individually. When problems change direction and increase in complexity, the teams pursuing them must grow in competencies. Below, I offer some remarkable examples that show how in entertainment, robotics, drug discovery, and banking, the best work is done in amoeba-like teams, casting out pseudopods in the direction of movement.

A young but wise Silicon Valley investor and client, Brian Flynn, once told me, "We find teams all over the world who want to compete in Silicon Valley, and they are fast and adaptive. The best ones are smart, creative, and eager to learn." Brian himself is a learning "junkie" who is always seeking to form teams and alliances that can take on juicy problems which, if solved, will make a significant difference.

A good leader rejects simple answers and, instead, works hard to find the right **questions**. Uncovering the right questions requires recruiting diverse teams, sharing knowledge, and learning together.

A "right question" causes us to work and to not settle for some bromide. Perhaps it's best to use an actual exchange to explain: Recently, I delivered a remote keynote talk from my location in San Francisco to 28 United Parcel Service (UPS) leaders who were gathered in Atlanta, Georgia. It delighted me to see the enthusiasm among this very diverse group of maturing leaders. They were working together to solve problems and improve their questions. The topic was "Curiosity and Learning." The session was kicked off with a nine-minute video in which Sharon Edelman, a wise and attractive television personality, asked me questions about learning companies. My partner, Yury Boshyk, was in Atlanta to direct learning exercises. Most of my time, for two and a half hours, was spent acting as "the question whisperer." To demonstrate the power of learning, I discussed four highly successful learning enterprises in remarkably different arenas:

- Pixar, a Northern California film company, was founded by Steve Jobs of Apple fame, as a part time venture. He wanted to show how, through the power of learning that combines technology, art, and filmmaking, a highly successful company would emerge. As you know, it worked.

- Unimerco, a Danish tool company, learned its way into being a global robotics solutions firm that rewarded all players with learning satisfactions, as well as very large paychecks.

- Sir James Black Lab, a small drug development lab in London, learned its way to solutions for irregular heartbeats (AFib) using beta blockers, and for stomach ulcers using Tagamet. Dr. Black was awarded a Nobel prize for his leadership.

- The Goldman Sachs Group, Inc. is a global investment banking, securities, and investment management company. They developed a learning center called Pine Street to answer the question, "Can upgrading the curiosity and learning of both bankers and their clients improve business?" It worked.

Although these organizations differ widely in size, type of business, and goals, they were all devoted to growing by learning—and they did. Now, years later, I was helping UPS get their questions right in order to boost their future business. But, in addition to this work, and writing a new book (this one), I also enjoyed my own learning opportunity: engaging with this lively group spanning various generations and backgrounds, who were interested in a wide array of curious issues.

With my admirable clients constantly pushing for upgraded questions and fresh applications of learning, I have a privileged role in helping them formulate questions, and I encourage their teams to address them. Here are some of the interesting questions that have emerged from this process:

- How can we employ artificial intelligence to expand our intellectual capabilities to better serve our customers?

- What can we do to help everyone we touch—customers, vendors, and partners—feel special and be more competent?

- How can each of us set learning goals and then find the resources to meet them?

- Where do we find our learning partners and cohorts to tackle the right questions?

WHAT TO LEARN:

In the highly complex, ever evolving, always ironic world of human development, there are no straight lines. All is in flux; all is continuously growing and decaying. It seems that the process of change generates the most growth.

For some of us, the prospect of learning, as our life's legacy, is most enticing and motivating. The questions surrounding legacy become more urgent as we descend the last mountain we have scaled. Many of my clients, having achieved success, turn more attention to what life is really all about as they reach the top of their current life learning curve.

The sad song, "Is That All There Is," famously sung by Peggy Lee,[16] poses the existential question we all need to face. We know that money is transitory, and our worldly goods wind up in the landfill. Can we leave behind curiosity and wonder? Might we diminish ignorance by promoting learning? Could our excitement for fresh questions and inquiries become the seed corn for the next generation?

The Five Acts

Countless holy texts, epic poems, and diaries show that humans are fascinated with the passage of time. In his personal journals, Roman Emperor Marcus Aurelius was one of the first to focus on the meaning of aging. He famously said, "It is not death that a man should fear; he should fear never beginning to live."[17] A very wise and more contemporary philosopher said it this way: "Age is a question of mind over matter; if you don't mind, it doesn't matter." (No one seems to be quite sure who actually originated this witticism, but it's been attributed to Mark Twain and Jack Benny, and as well as Satchel Paige, a baseball Hall of Famer and endurance phenomenon who pitched until he was 57!)[18]

In the social sciences, there is a longstanding tradition of studying lives in stages. There are, arguably, five transitions adults must make in coping with each adult life stage. Erik Erickson, Jean Piaget, Lawrence Kohlberg, Roger Gould, and Daniel Levinson—all heroic researchers in the area of human development—plowed through mountains of data and interviewed people in each stage. Writers like Bill Bridges and Gail Sheehy became devoted popularizers of the notion that life has distinct stages. Bridges was a professor of English who became interested in the power of storytelling and mythology in human development. He authored *Transitions*, a guide written for laypeople caught up in the challenges of navigating adult development.[19] Sheehy borrowed heavily from social science research in writing her well-known book *Passages*, which inspires readers to see the predictable crises of adult life as opportunities for growth.[20] I have followed this time-honored path by presenting my personal adult-life drama in five stages, or "acts," as I've termed them. In creating this guidebook, I have borrowed shamelessly from these scholars' collective efforts (with high purpose, of course).

It's not only academics who want to apply frameworks to their observations about how life is to be lived at each stage. Emperor Frederick the Great, who ruled Prussia from 1740-1786, needed a specific number to calculate how much funding to set aside for retirement payouts, so he set the retirement age for civil servants at 60. In this arbitrary way, the length of the "working years" was determined.

And today, commerce is blatantly clear in its use of life's transitions to sell goods. "Wearing your father's jeans" is a big put-down. What's good for a Baby Boomer is anathema to a Gen-Xer or Gen-Zer. That goes for music, technical devices, TV shows, and, of course, social media. Upon every act of life, commerce bestows labels, expectations and sales targets. But individuals should not allow arbitrary dates to govern their actions or learning.

I will describe my own classification of the five adult-life stages (acts) a bit later, but the general rationale I use to define them is based on how we learn and what we are required to learn in each stage. I've tried to think of life stages as long learning curves. While my breakdown is based partially on the academic schemes of sociologists and psychologists, I've also considered themes from science and the arts.

An example of science figuring into my reckoning is how Jonas Salk, one of my mentors and teachers, helped me understand the power of learning curves and entropy. In his book *Survival of the Wisest*, he describes the critical importance of our changing learning curves when entropy begins to drag upon them.[21] Salk, who discovered the

Salk vaccine for polio, was ever the scientist. He grew colonies of fruit flies in an enclosed environment, then observed these lowly creatures begin to reduce their breeding to match the limits imposed by their circumstances. Would that humans could be so mindful.

The art of theater has offered a longstanding learning method for many cultures. We are still learning about human nature from the ancient Greek plays *Oedipus Rex, Antigone,* and *Medea* by Sophocles and Euripides. These enduring dramas inform us about our humanness: the good, the bad, and the ugly. In more recent times, we've had William Shakespeare, Henrik Ibsen, Leo Tolstoy, Arthur Miller, and many other playwrights to help us understand basic human drives and growth trajectories.

Great theater always begins with compelling questions that get resolved, act by act, as we, the audience, learn more and more:

- Who done it?

- Will love prevail?

- Can this marriage survive?

- When will Godot arrive?

I like the image of our own dramatic acts unfolding around big, unresolved questions. As in the art of the drama or the challenge of science, each of us must generate our own compelling questions. Each stage demands new material, age-appropriate stories, wise advisors, kind supporters, travel mates, and decent critics. My intention in this book is to help readers examine what's needed in each act in order to cope—and to keep smiles on their faces.

Below is a peek at how I've chosen to define each adult-stage act. Some of my efforts to navigate from one act to another are rational;

others not so much:

Act I: Early Adulthood [Planning and Packing]
⋯ Age 18 ~ 35 ⋯

All journeys need preparation. It helps if a veteran traveler reviews our intentions and advises on what not to pack. The poems in this section are dedicated to John Levy, the former executive director of the San Francisco-based Jung Institute. He taught me many things including how to travel lightly, both physically and mentally. He earned both an Electrical Engineering degree and an MBA from Stanford, but he became a wise man by learning how to get properly lost, enjoy the moment, recover, and renew.

Act II: Staying on the Path [While Occasionally Getting Lost]
⋯ Age 35 ~ 50 ⋯

In the *Iliad* and the *Odyssey*, Homer's Odysseus suffered serious distractions and seductions before returning on course.[22] Once launched on the journey, youthful energy and resources are vital. A "flow state" wherein talents and competence match challenges is ideal. Between such flow states, maintenance, keeping score, and tracking progress are needed. Caveat emptor: Some of this can be truly boring stuff—humor is required.

Act III: Taking Stock [And Reprovisioning]
⋯ Age 50 ~ 65 ⋯

To continue in flow, that lovely near-euphoric state in which time stands still, a new learning curve must be found as the old one loses power. As energy diminishes, frustration rises. At this point, fresh advisors and sources of fuel must be found to meet new challenges. Again, please remember: Mix all new fuel with laughter. John Levy's fuel sources always included good wine, delicious food, and humor.

Act IV: Curioser and Curioser [Going Deeper into Life]
⋯ Age 65 ~ 80 ⋯

By this stage, you have learned to be a good observer of your needs and to discern the ways in which you must change to meet the next learning challenge. What might have been appropriate in earlier stages will be counterproductive in the near-summary act, the denouement. Once again, fresh, act-appropriate guides and role models are required. At this stage, it may be tempting to cling to what worked earlier. Don't! Or, it may seem too big a leap, therefore a lunge in a new direction is required. It's not! Like Alice,[23] let your curiosity take you on a brand new learning adventure.

Act V: Bonus Years [A La Mode]
⋯ Age 80 ~ Who Knows? ⋯

If you made it through the previous acts still self-propelling, curious, reading, enjoying good conversations, music, and doing even one thing that contributes to the common good, then you have won the trifecta. The banquet reaches the dolce vita stage as vanity is tamed and the senses are calmed. "Of course, I will have the ice cream." "Let me try my hand at writing hip hop." You can invent your own sense of style. You can be generous, since holding onto things raises the question: "For what?" The right questions to consider may be:

- Who do I want at my banquet?

- What help do I need to pull it off?

- How do I select the menu?

Fortunately, in the Bonus Years, people can learn from the generations behind them. A group of Gen-Xers started a program called "The Dinner Party" to get people of their generation together who have suffered losses and feel alone in their grieving. I met with the leaders of this movement, and I am sure they could help Bonus Years people get organized to support one another, too. It must be that way for sapiens to robustly survive and continue to contribute.

|||||||||||||||||||||||||||||||||||||||||||||||||||||||||||||||||||||||||||||||||||||||||||||||||||||||||||||||||||||||||||||||||||||||||||||||||||||||||||||||||||||||||||||

WHAT TO LEARN:

Like unfolding acts in a drama, each of life's stages brings fresh challenges, new characters, tension, humor, and uncertainty. Flashbacks often open up possibilities for character development and plot enrichment. Think of these transitional stages as acts in a drama, connected but discrete. Examining each act will help us sharpen our understanding of the next.

|||||||||||||||||||||||||||||||||||||||||||||||||||||||||||||||||||||||||||||||||||||||||||||||||||||||||||||||||||||||||||||||||||||||||||||||||||||||||||||||||||||||||||||

Please remember: In each of life's acts, action and humor must come into play. It may be said that most of life is about observing, choosing opportunities to pursue, preparing, finding paths forward, prat-falling, and then recovering. Many of us have followed that same process in a myriad of ways, and it all goes better with humor. Comedian Jack Benny decided he wanted to remain forever 39. It became a long running gag, proving that denying aging can be very funny. Benny made a fortune doing it.

The following chapters on each act include commentary on the obstacles one typically encounters, profiles of people who tackled them in creative ways, and even rap poems intended to bring smiles. Each life stage, or act, inspired me to write particular poems or, as my poet friend Michael Wolfe calls them, "musings." I hope they help capture grins while my readers are languishing in, plodding through, or enjoying each particular act.

ACT I

EARLY ADULTHOOD
[PLANNING AND PACKING]

··· AGE 18-35 ···

Can we pack good karma? It's needed in abundance in this stage. Why? Life development and early adulthood begin with high hopes and hidden doubts—lots of them. Fears must be tamped down, and a determined persona must be developed.

Young adulthood can be many things for each of us: reckless adventuring, rigorous training, planning (or winging it), extending adolescence, dreaming of jackpots, and going public. Good teachers and wise mentors are needed to help us wade through this stage. My personal favorite Act 1 hero journey stories are the Arthurian legends. In his delight-filled book *The Once and Future King*, author T.H. White shows us how Merlin, the magician and mentor, teaches the young king how to conduct a proper learning journey. Here's one snippet of Merlin's advice: "The best thing for being sad ... is to learn something. That is the only thing that never fails."[24]

Here are some common requirements for a successful young adulthood:

- Be able to articulate a plan. (This is necessary to answer adults' prying questions about your "life goals.")

- Affect a style. (Which way to wear your baseball cap?)

- Find proper (fun) companions and coaches to learn the basic strategy of recovering your dignity when you step on a banana peel or something even smellier, because life in this stage is littered with banana peels.

- Learn for the gratification itself and not for today's tweet.

Teachers, Mentors, Character Shapers, and Wisdom Carriers

It is certainly not uncommon for young adults to drag out their early developmental years. Turning the baseball cap backward, hanging with friends, living at home, and keeping ear buds pumping the latest music all seem to be common practices.

No journey through young adulthood would be complete without exploring spiritual caverns, making lists (lots of them), going on "walkabouts," and, of course, deconstructing heroes like Apple founder Steve Jobs. Obviously, journeys are vastly different for those in wartime or those living life on the edge, whether fiscally or physically.

Let's take a look at how several remarkable people helped me navigate young adulthood.

Rollo Jones, Teacher and Mentor

If you're lucky as a young person, you come across a teacher who makes you curious about learning and somehow honors you in the effort. Rollo Jones, one of my high school English teachers, sported pink paisley ties with his custom-tailored blue blazer, in a school populated by black-robed Jesuits. He wore elegant rings and a gold Rolex watch and he loved poetry, theater, opera, and classical literature. He took us on jaunts to San Francisco to experience the symphony, opera, and theater.

Rollo's greatest gift was his ability to honor students so that each felt recognized, even while we were making hash out of Walt Whitman, Henry Wadsworth Longfellow, Charles Dickens, or Robert Frost. He organized a Saturday morning radio show that students wrote, directed, and performed. We learned the art of sound effects: cannons booming (a sheet of steel and a wooden mallet) and horse hooves thundering (coconut shells).

I was paired with Rollo's favorite student, Norman Berryessa, easily the most attractive in the school's population of 1,400. Norman was handsome, polite, smart, and always had the stunning Shirley, the prettiest girl in our small town, on his arm at school dances. He was a crooner (Perry Como-style) and was a lead in our school plays. Being assigned to write the radio shows elevated my status, especially since Norman was involved.

Rollo taught us to respect and enjoy good writing and beautiful sounds and sights. He showed us art prints by French Impressionists and Dutch Masters. At first, we faked interest to please him, but then some of us felt the aesthetic pull. His own open passion for the arts was contagious, but his real power was in his excitement about our learning. Even the class-clown-student-jock Wayne Bellarde (later drafted by the Yankees) got Rollo's approbation for his reading of the poem "Casey at the Bat."

Bellarmine, an all-boys prep school, was known for high standards and firm discipline. Father Rooney, Prefect of Discipline, was not averse to using his six-foot-three frame to shape us up. Rollo, the slightly pudgy dandy, really stood out. And, looking back, I believe it took considerable courage for him just to be himself. He didn't know that I was the only non-Catholic boy out of 1,400. He just accepted who I was. Maybe that's what a great teacher does: he makes us appreciate who we might become by gently honoring our early sprouts. What a lasting gift.

WHAT TO LEARN:

It's curious just how early our "early adulthood" begins. The half-life of math and science education can be very short. But aesthetics and liberal arts education can grow in depth and satisfaction over time, especially if planted in good soil during adolescence. From

Rollo I learned the power, contagion, and excitement of learning and remaining true to oneself. This is not to say that our passion for learning—of all types—may not depreciate: Of course it does. John Gardner, former Secretary of Health, Education, and Welfare, and president of the Carnegie Corporation, vividly illustrated this risk of decay with his root-bound image of needing to find a new pot for fresh growth, in his brilliant book, *Self-Renewal.*[25]

Jonas Salk, Wisdom Carrier

Jonas Salk was tough. The American researcher and virologist was, first of all, tough on himself. He fretted about being obsolete. When I was still at AT&T in New York, we were introduced by mutual friends, then got together to discuss intellectual development. After our first meeting, I agreed to serve on the board of his foundation. It was Salk who taught me that learning had a very short half-life, especially in science. He divided learning into Epoch A and Epoch B. In this scheme, what we know today is in Epoch A, but it will be useless or, worse, counterproductive in Epoch B. He believed that we are always falling behind because we cling to our beliefs, especially to the beliefs that once brought us success. Physicist, historian, and philosopher of science, Thomas Kuhn, effectively explicated and popularized this concept when he coined the term "paradigm shift" in his book, *The Structure of Scientific Revolutions.*[26]

Ever the scientist, Salk backed up his Epoch A-B theory through a series of experiments with fruit flies that demonstrate how they balance their breeding patterns to match the size of their environment and available resources. Imagine that! Wild stuff that the world should learn immediately, as I alluded to in "Setting the Stage." Salk presented this idea philosophically as a prescription for humanity, in his book *Survival of the Wisest,*[27] which also bolsters author and public servant

John Gardner's advice about repotting.

Of course, Salk was widely known: He gained enormous fame for his polio vaccine, which came into use in 1955. The World Health Organization lists it as an essential medicine and its use, along with the Sabin oral version, reduced cases of polio from 350,000 in 1988 to 359 in 2014. He later shifted to another scientific puzzle—AIDS—which he failed to solve. He was using his Epoch A work on vaccines to tackle AIDS, which proved to be a very different Epoch B problem. With his tremendous energy, well-earned celebrity, and as a result of tireless fund-raising through such initiatives as the March of Dimes, Salk assembled top people to begin new explorations in the life sciences. He founded the Salk Institute in La Jolla, California and began attacking other health problems.

He also grew more philosophical and spent less and less time in the lab. Fortunately, he took up art, painting mostly, at the right time. It sustained the creative half of his life. A muse came along, Françoise Gilot, who had been Picasso's last mistress and mother of two of his children. Gilot enchanted Salk, a kid from Brooklyn, drawing him into art and into his right brain. It was lovely to watch him being reborn.

WHAT TO LEARN:

Teachers help us see what lies ahead or at least help to sort out the prospects of tomorrow. My learning from Jonas Salk helped me rethink my own life assumptions and consider what nuggets of value I could build into my first book, *Paradox of Success*. The best guides help elevate curiosity. My last visit with Jonas was on the beach in La Jolla, where he was scribbling down ideas for solving AIDS. When I saw his intensity, I wished him success and moved on.

Eleanor Roosevelt, Character Shaper

Young adults are often blasé or effect "cool," whatever the current definition of that word may be. But when you meet someone whom your family has placed on a very high pedestal, you may find yourself melting, or worse. For me, this happened on a warm summer evening at the Manhattan residence of Adlai Stevenson, then US Ambassador to the United Nations. It was the time of the 1964 Democratic Convention in Atlantic City, where Lyndon Johnson would be picked to battle Barry Goldwater.

At AT&T headquarters, I had quietly been anointed as the "house Democrat," since I knew California Governor Pat Brown (his family were friends of mine). It seemed like a stretch to me, but there were very few "out" Democrats at AT&T (that's a story for another time). So I was selected to attend the get-together of Democrats at Stevenson's home. When I arrived (on time, of course), I was amazed when the ambassador himself opened the door. He escorted me into a small gathering, with Eleanor Roosevelt at its center, and introduced me. The lady smiled warmly and patted the seat next to her. For the next hour, I got the full-charm press, with lots of well-constructed questions. She seemed terribly interested in a range of topics—from open housing (then on the California ballot), to food, to women's issues.

Mrs. Roosevelt's questions were so well constructed that she could weave them effortlessly into an ongoing conversation, while obtaining the information she sought. She was especially curious about the way women and girls were treated and the roadblocks they faced. Since my family had been close to and supportive of Helen Gahagan Douglas, a progressive Congressional representative from our district in California, I could give her first-hand impressions. She also wanted my take on Richard Nixon, who had attacked Douglas as a Soviet sympathizer. Mrs. Roosevelt seemed fascinated with Nixon, as one might be fascinated by a coiled rattlesnake.

When I left the party, that night, I walked all the way to my apartment in Greenwich Village, thinking about the power and grace of this woman. I second-guessed my responses and the things I might have said but didn't. My feelings were intense; sleep, I suspected, would be elusive. I said a short walking prayer of gratitude for all the privileges I enjoyed that had gotten me to that gathering. I began to recalibrate my future plans. Curiously, when I did get to bed, I crashed.

||||||||||||||||||||||||||||||||||||||||||||||||||||||||||||||||||||||||||||||||||||||||||||||||||||||||||||||||||||||||||||||||||||||||||||||||||||||||||||||||||||||||

W H A T   T O   L E A R N :

In a very short time, I received lessons I've never forgotten: Design questions so that both sender and receiver can learn, listen intensely to each answer, and follow up. That's how learning grows. Select topics you really care about and prompt the person answering to deliver rich responses. Always remember: It's not about you! The person you're addressing must feel honored by the attention the question elicits. Be warm and kind to younger people, and bloody well learn from them! Oh, and by the way, I asked Mrs. Roosevelt only two questions: What readings she would recommend, and if she liked jazz. She loved jazz great Louis Armstrong, and she got me to read Edward Gibbon's *The History of the Decline and Fall of the Roman Empire.*

||||||||||||||||||||||||||||||||||||||||||||||||||||||||||||||||||||||||||||||||||||||||||||||||||||||||||||||||||||||||||||||||||||||||||||||||||||||||||||||||||||||||

Golda O'Neil, Character Shaper and Teacher

Along the road to finding common characteristics in a diverse group of men and women who remained highly productive across their entire lifespans, I fell into a surprising insight: There were, in fact, common strands of beliefs and characteristics running through their lives. It can be difficult to see the common elements, because history focuses on their achievements, but it seems that courses are set in our early days, as psychologist Abraham Maslow suggested.

Extraordinary people are usually studied one by one, by biographers or historians or even novelists: a great scientist here; a wildly prolific artist there; political, business, and military leaders everywhere. Few fools have attempted to get to the common fuel that ignites all of them, let alone the common purposes or ethics they might share. I call the common element the "elixir factor." It's the sweet, savory fuel of the gods—our essence. My mother, Golda, created her own taxonomy: "Ordinary people care about things; educated people care about ideas; and extraordinary people follow their ideals." The elixir factor is all about remaining "learning hungry" and true to your ideals.

I recall hearing Golda's dictum on learning when I was very young (maybe nine), as a reason to avoid accumulating stuff. During the Depression, that was an especially relevant ethic. Besides, if you did pursue things you were ordinary, and that was to be avoided. Was Golda a snob? In some ways, yes.

By sheer Depression Era economics, Golda was forced to be an autodidact. She had to leave Stanford to go to work teaching in a one-room school in frigid, rural Utah, while helping to care for the miserable family farm. She also supported a brood of brothers and sisters, who had gone off to war or college, only to return home after finding that there were few jobs to be had. I can easily imagine Golda retreating, every spare minute, into her literary world of ideas and ideals: Ralph Waldo Emerson, Walt Whitman, Alfred Lord Tennyson, Emily Dickenson, William Shakespeare, Samuel Clements, Will Rogers. Good literature and dreams of better days kept her fire of idealism burning. One of her favorite poets, Edna St. Vincent Millay, wrote, "My candle burns at both ends/ It will not last the night/ but, ah my foes and oh my friends/ it gives a lovely light."[28] The poem aptly describes Golda's struggle.

A curious aspect of Golda's life was that she avoided any religious affiliation, especially Jewish connections. Religion would come later for her. As a young woman she led, rather surprisingly, a "flapper life." Her leaving Stanford was probably about a lack of funds, but she had also been arrested by "those Palo Alto bluenose police" for wearing her dancing bloomers on public streets. She was in a dance group that specialized in stuff as scandalous as the Black Bottom, the Charleston, and the Shimmy. Racy indeed, but also an expression of her personal freedom—an ideal she hammered into her children. Golda had a rebellious gene—a streak of independence that would serve her family well, later on.

<hr />

WHAT TO LEARN:

Golda was hungry to learn. We lived in the desert, a harsh place that would occasionally bloom and become beautiful. She tried to make sure that we lived with other kinds of beauty, as well. She learned from the beauty that writers and poets create, while she helped to fashion a working ranch raising dates and grapefruit. Even though these were cash crops, Golda felt she was creating an aesthetic oasis—and the ranch became one in our imaginations. My father, an alcoholic, retreated, letting my mother have her way. But he admired what she did and supported her. Our lives become a learning oasis filled, with aesthetic and intellectual wonders, in the middle of a harsh desert.

<hr />

J. D. Salinger, Wisdom Carrier

In his novel, *The Catcher in the Rye*, J. D. Salinger captured the general cynicism of young people teetering on the edge of adulthood. The language was perfect in its critical tone toward adults, who were mostly written off as bumbling, insincere fools—and certainly not presented as models to emulate. The following exchange, for example, between Holden, our hero, and Spencer, a smarmy representative of the establishment, delighted readers everywhere:

Spencer: "Life is a game, boy. Life is a game one plays according to the rules."

Holden: "Yes sir. I know it is. I know it."

Holden to himself: "Game my ass. Some game. If you get on the side where all the hot-shots are, then it's a game, all right—I'll admit that. But if you get on the other side, where there aren't any hot-shots, then what's a game about? Nothing. No game."[29]

WHAT TO LEARN:

A healthy dose of skepticism is needed to enter what Salinger calls "the game." The positive takeaway of Holden's cynicism is the clarity that things are never as they're represented by the people who hold the power. The negative lesson is that carrying doubt, anger, and cynicism can be damaging if they're allowed to simmer in the shadows of the unconscious. Our job, therefore, is to see as clearly as possible what lies ahead and not be damaged either by unconsciously entering "the game" or by never really engaging life at all.

Readings for Act I

For more inspiration on navigating the stages of life, I offer some suggested readings that are rewarding on their own terms, but also may serve to help you make the right choices wherever your life journey is taking you. The list that follows is especially relevant to young adulthood.

- *The Once and Future King* by T. H. White—This well-told tale is funny and right on target in all respects, especially Merlin's teachings and young Arthur's failings.[30]

- *The Works of King Arthur and His Noble Knights* by John Steinbeck— A charming visit to the sites where King Arthur allegedly lived and ruled shows this great writer's respect for the legends.[31]

- *The Iliad* and *The Odyssey* by Homer—This great Greek poet nails his hero's journey and the elements of all of life's adventures.[32]

- *The Catcher in the Rye* by J. D. Salinger—This American classic spells out the many stresses of growing into adulthood when all of the adults around you don't "get it." This is an essential book for the backpack on all life journeys.[33]

- *Siddhartha* by Hermann Hesse—This amazing life-navigation guide, based on stories of the Buddha's life adventures, won Hesse a Nobel Prize. A young aristocrat in India must set off on a discovery quest: gaining riches, having a mistress, searching for his "tribe," losing ground, then finding resolution in service and simplicity. What a tale well told![34]

- *Don Quixote* by Miguel de Cervantes—One of the most important literary adventure tales ever written, this novel deals with a poor farmer's quest for fame and fortune. The reader must decide who this nameless hidalgo really is and what this bizarre journey is really about (a tough but rewarding read).[35]

POEMS
FOR YOUNG ADULTHOOD

The poems in this section are inspired by the wondrous possibilities and dreads that young adulthood presents. They examine how the best of plans wander off and how getting lost can be the best part of the adventure. After all, life is all about exploration, and the side roads are where the action often lies. In scrambling and recovering, the hero's journey gets really interesting and learning prizes are won. Young adults try out life in many off-road ways, like going on juice diets or exhorting kale. The poems celebrate them all.

After reading the poems in this section, you may wish to do a quick inventory of your own needs and those of friends and loved ones you may be called upon to help. Remember that failures in each life stage must be revisited until they're set right—even if that's never!

Looking for My Tribe

Decided to get a cool handle to tweet
but not sure where my tribe lives—
Facebook, LinkedIn, match.com?
Tried places where people
showed parts better left covered.

Saw where a politician
showed off his pride and joy,
but the voters didn't approve.
A bit later his career drooped;
he suffered a rise and fall.

Spengler spent years studying Romans;
their social networks had latrines
where they displayed Roman power
while bathing.

Whatever happened to empire?
Was it a bad concept?
Can we do better with Xboxes?
Ask "Miss Thumbs." She gets her tribe,
and she has a lovely handle:
Digit Power.

My tribal leader, Jon Stewart, is tired.
Not enough sleep, he claims, with tweets.
But his blog will get the big-thumbers,
Can I join?
Will we start a new empire?

The Journey Ahead

That fork in the road—are you sure it's there?
I don't see where it forks—
is there a sign?

Good travelers look around for top value.
Not for road forks, though.
Maybe a field of happy red poppies will appear,
or smiling sunflowers will enchant.

Don't make your travel plans too grand.
Odysseus did; it backfired.

My friend John Levy said it best:
"Practice getting lost;
every small road in France is worth taking."
His advice led to lots of good wine and good food.

Lose the Michelin and its
fussy ways.
Your nose will lead you to John's heaven:
Heed the siren call of sautéed garlic.
Was it escargots Odysseus sought?
Frost would have us not dither
over roads not taken
Just take the fragrant one,
and enjoy!

On Planning

General George Marshall said, "Plans are nothing, but
planning is everything," and he won
World War II and a Nobel Prize.
That's good enough for common folk
planning a good life.

No great warrior but a helluva planner am I.
Let's see—lunch next week.
Is Wednesday open?
What week is that? I need to know for planning purposes.

Can you imagine worse plans than written ones?
Can you smell the rot of decaying assumptions?
Can we keep from giggling when Congress
pompously proclaims its plans?

God gave us lovely planless birds
who build nests—
each twig laid perfectly—
no blueprint!
Now consider all the Chinese
building lots of stuff.

Will they follow the birds or
a grand plan?
Progress has eaten their birds' habitat;
it's gone.
Let's make a plan to put it back.
A lovely birdsong to start?
Let's ask God for a plan.

He needs a giggle, the joke goes.

Kale, the Fuel

The best jokes are mysterious,
like kale.
Who invented this strange veggie
that must be beaten to be eaten?

Being a health-conscious regularity guy,
I lean toward roughage—
no white bread, please—
fruits yes, cabbage maybe, but
cleanses never.

I read a health magazine once and suffered;
couldn't eat for two weeks without pain.
Too many beans and too much kale.
It seems I neglected my Beano
and didn't chew my kale sufficiently.

I stopped reading such dangerous material;
felt better then and there.
Until a visit with Jack LaLanne, him all
sweaty and earnest.

He asked me to help him pull a train
with my teeth. Imagine!
I demurred.
"I haven't had my kale," I said.
He replied: "Use my juicer, like on TV.
It whips kale into submission!"

ACT II

STAYING ON THE PATH
[WHILE OCCASIONALLY GETTING LOST]

··· AGE 35-50 ···

The beginning of what is called "midlife" may be merely the point when the benefits of earlier journeys are harvested. In young adulthood, experimentation is the key—trying various paths and back alleys, getting lost and being found. But all that experience is supposed to ripen and be harvested in Act II.

The right path—variously described as a groove (like a golf swing), a steep learning curve, and getting into "the flow"—is that time in one's life when acquiring competence is sought to match the right challenge. And, as the challenge is heightened, competency must be elevated to match it. Mihaly Csikszentmihalyi, a brilliant research psychologist, discovered "flow" states—with surgeons, basketball players, bike riders, and other groups—moments when every challenge is met with the right responses and time seems to stand still. Basketball superstar Michael Jordan described his flow state by saying: "We all fly. Once you leave the ground, you fly."[37] Boxing legend Muhammad Ali touted the importance of flow with his indelible words: "Float like a butterfly, sting like a bee. The hands can't hit what the eyes can't see."[38]

Much has been written about the midlife crisis, when identity itself is being threatened. But the transition leading up to the mid-years is equally fraught. The period of the mid-30s to late 40s is characterized by:

- High energy and rapid learning
- Focused drive and productivity
- Intermittent flow states

- Achievements and failures

- Establishing family

- Being adored by marketers as a big spender in a big demographic

Act II contains three big hazards that await the ill prepared, and that is most of us. I wrote about these potential hazards in my book, *The Paradox of Success*. Here they are:

- The biggest trap in Act II is either going forward without a top-notch guide or following a faker. The Greeks called false wise men "Sophists." Today's Sophists are most likely to be Web or TV personalities. They all sound sincere and clever, but they sell fake goods. A true mentor or guide helps us frame proper questions and pursue healthy and dynamic learning paths.

- The second-biggest trap comes from the blinding aspects of success. The wisdom of ancient Greek mythology revealed the destructive aspects of hubris, or overweening pride: poor Icarus, the lad who tried to fly to the sun only to come crashing down into the sea, and his father Daedalus, who had to watch his son perish for affronting the gods by flying too close to the sun with the meltable wings he had invented.

- The third-biggest trap is failing to learn from errors, and instead covering them over or rushing past the lessons inherent in these mistakes. Put positively, the right learning comes from decent failures. Act II may be suffused with flops that result from risking new ventures and exploring incipient creative capabilities. We might once turn again to Michael Jordan, who in his wisdom confessed, "I have failed over and over and over in my life and that is why I succeeded."[39]

Character Shapers and Wisdom Carriers

John Gardner, Character Shaper

Expert at making behavioral science research clear and useful, political commentator David Brooks knows how to pick interesting topics. For his March 22, 2016 *New York Times* column, Brooks chose to debunk the so-called midlife crisis. Based on the research in a book called *Life Reimagined* by Barbara Bradley Hagerty,[40] he points out that the celebrated midlife crisis is more a matter of shifting gears than of acquiring a red convertible sports car. According to Brooks: "Midlife begins to seem like the second big phase of decision making. Your identity has been formed; you know who you are; you've built up your resources; and now you have the chance to take the big risks precisely because your foundation is already secure."[41]

In his book, *Self-Renewal*, my mentor, John Gardner, talked about "repotting,"[42] or finding more room for your roots to grow. Gardner's own life was a series of growth moves, not necessarily upward. He taught psychology after a career as an intelligence officer during World War II. He became president of the Carnegie Corporation to satisfy his curiosity and extend his reach in education. He became Secretary of Health, Education and Welfare under President Lyndon Johnson, quietly helping to shape Civil Rights legislation and to create Common Cause and the White House Fellows program.

Throughout his various "growth" assignments John had time to nudge and support mentees like me. His style was marvelous: He would call and say, "I am at the Fairmont Hotel. Can I escape and meet you?" I always said, "Yes," and we'd walk and talk. His opening question was always, "What have you learned since I last saw you?" I was always prepared to answer.

One day, John called and surprised me by saying, "I'm thinking about another change. Would you help me?" He was feeling a strong need to "repot." Washington, for him, had become poor soil for any real growth. We discussed his returning to teaching at Stanford or Berkeley (he chose Stanford). John wanted to teach leadership to undergraduates, as well as explore the bigger questions about life and how to live it properly. He wanted to write and think about the subject from a fresh perch. So, he did.

David Brooks concluded his column about the virtues of midlife transition with these words: "They achieve a kind of tranquility, not because they decided to do nothing, but because they have achieved focus and purity of will."[43] That was true for John Gardner. He no longer needed the pomp and power diet that Washington lives on.

It's curious that Brooks, a more recent student of and writer on the subject of character, would follow my dear friend and mentor, John Gardner, down the road to renewal. For many people, the idea of shifting four gears to achieve the rewards of transition is both daunting and exciting. But it beats the hell out of a red sports car! I know, because I had a red MG and developed a close and costly relationship with my mechanic. His name was Reginald and he always had a great smile and a warm greeting when I showed up with wallet in hand.

———

WHAT TO LEARN:

Occasionally, we meet people who inspire us by their life example, as well as their thoughts. John Gardner was such a person. As one of John's mentees, I had to raise my sights and examine my assumptions about what it means to live a proper, productive life. "What have you learned since we last met?" His question is still with me.

———

Gordie Sherman, Character Shaper

One Sunday morning, I received a call from Gordie Sherman, the former president of Midas International. I knew immediately from his deep bass voice who it was. "John, I have news," he said. "I'm moving out of Chicago and will become your neighbor in Mill Valley. I have a new challenge—leukemia. The doctors here gave me six months, so I fired them. I'm searching for a new team. I will need your help." His strong voice and flat affect made the news less shocking. And I merely said, "Of course, Gordie. We'll get started whenever you say." I hung up and sobbed.

With the help of his new medical team at the University of California, San Francisco, the months originally given to Gordie were stretched into years of great living. Each month, we would meet for an Italian meal and celebrate the latest news from the blood tests. Gordie taught me how to fly fish at his fishing lodge on a sacred stream. Between trips to the river, we learned to cook while listening to opera and Shakespeare. Gordie refused to become effete: He learned to play bagpipe and oboe. He began to teach music appreciation at the San Francisco Conservatory. He raised orchids. On one occasion, a woman visitor gushing over the orchids asked, "May I touch them?" Gordie laughed and said, "You can fuck 'em if you like."

With others, Gordie and I helped form a group called Business Executives Move for Vietnam Peace. Our mission was to lobby Congress to stop the war. I was still at AT&T and had done some lobbying (with checkbook for "events"). I was welcome on both sides of the aisle. These efforts were making a difference, and my kids thought I was cool. My efforts were not enthusiastically received at AT&T headquarters, and I made Nixon's enemy list, which was very cool but a bloody pain.

Gordie, who outran his disease, once said, "Dying is a wonderful way to live if it doesn't kill you." He squeezed every drop of life from every day. Laughing, playing with his dogs, taking lots of pictures of "the rear ends of ducks," he plowed on for 12 more lovely years after his initial prognosis, and generously took me along for the ride.

WHAT TO LEARN:

Life is not about time management. It's is about our use of time. It's about being brave. Because Gordie refused to be chained to his disease, he followed his doctors' advice, but lived fully. He never stopped learning and living with gusto. He and French Renaissance philosopher Michel de Montaigne would have made great comrades following Greek philosopher Epicurus down a happy road pursuing the good life (more on Montaigne later).

John Levy, Character Shaper

John Levy's family were among the pioneering Jews who settled in San Francisco and formed companies like Levi Strauss. I've known very few heirs who have managed their money as well as John Levy. He gave most of it away. But he was wise, and he gave his wisdom along with the money. John grew up in a privileged household. He was discriminated against as a Jew. His answer: Become a heavyweight boxer. His nose never forgave him. He loved to laugh, and that's where I came in. I was a sucker for John's bad jokes.

After a stint in the Navy and at Bechtel Engineering, John turned to his favorite topics: lovely women and psychology. I was doing the same double major. When I became president of the California School of Professional Psychology (CSPP), several people told me I must meet John Levy. We met and we never stopped meeting. John helped me find Joe Henderson, the preeminent Jungian analyst with whom I worked on my own healing and transition.

A string of bright, wonderful people appeared in my life because of John. Among them were pioneers of humanistic psychology and avant-garde thinking: Roger Walsh, author and professor of medicine; Frances Vaughn, psychologist and author; Rollo May, widely read psychotherapist; Jim Bugental, one of the founders of humanistic psychology; Tony Athos, writer and Harvard Business School professor; George Harris, editor at the *Harvard Business Review*; Michael Murphy, scholar, writer, and founder of Esalen; and Angie Arrien, the multitalented anthropologist, writer, and religious leader of the Basques.

For a while, I searched for "Eastern wisdom" through creativity and meditation. I created a meditation platform with tatami mats, brewed endless cups of green tea, studied Aikido (and wrote about it), and practiced writing haiku. In the end, it was writing about my experiences and life lessons that truly allowed me to exercise my creativity.

John was generous in many ways, and his affirmations never flagged. I would show him a clay trophy and he would smile. A sad flower arrangement brought enough praise to keep me going. In the meantime, his epicurean spirit was supported by his generous and inspired Alsatian-style cooking. An invitation to his dinner parties was a perfect poultice for my creative wounds. Selfishly, I gave him a copy of Julia Child's book on French cooking. It paid great dividends.

John's biggest gift was a generosity of heart. Adele, his lover-wife who kept him inspired and happy, also became a close friend. John never stopped giving. A book, a prayer, a joke (sometimes really bad ones)—all would come unbidden if he thought you'd like it. He offered his advice to many people—young and old—and yet was never pedantic. His kindness and generosity allowed him to go through life unburdened by things—he simply passed them on. He helped shape the character of many people, including mine, fortunately.

WHAT TO LEARN:

Laugh. It's not that serious. Be generous, with both time and things. We have too much stuff, and besides, sharing somehow gives us something more. Be bawdy—enjoy every meal and sip of wine. Always take the road that leads to good food and loving company.

Angeles Arrien, Character Shaper

Imagine meeting an important teacher, a healer, standing diminutively at your door on your 50th birthday. That's how I met Angeles Arrien, the dark-eyed, well-formed, young woman we called Angie. She was a "gift" from my friend John Levy. Angie's task, as she put it, was to help me plan the second half of my life.

Angie came armed with bonhomie and tarot cards. We set about the work after I ushered her to the dining room table and got her tea and water. With facile digits and a reassuring smile, she turned over the cards. In a calm, professional voice, Angie explained the archetypal figures as they appeared. Never rushed, she explained how the archetypes play out in life's third act.

Angie had the gracious authority befitting a spiritual leader of the Basques (an indigenous people of Spain). She followed her father in the powerful role of serving the Basques in diaspora in Europe and the US. Modestly, she kept her PhD in Cultural Anthropology from UC Berkeley in the background. She dressed professionally: aqua blue shirt and grey skirt, nothing fussy, no makeup, and as a bona fide Sausalito houseboat dweller, she wore sandals.

Angie was a kind and gracious person with strong empathic powers. Although she had no way of knowing it, I had been studying archetypes going back to early Greek mythology and ancient Asian art with Jungian analyst Joe Henderson. Her tarot reading made for a lovely synchronicity of learning. For Angie, the cards were keys that evoked searching conversations about the shape and purpose of preparing for the second half of life. Using the magic of the ancient images, we talked about the nature of learning that lay ahead: Each of us must allow early ambition and power-seeking to give way to a deeper inner life and creativity.

There are birthday presents that delight us, but Angie offered a gift that grew in its power of transformation; it kept shaping me in mysterious ways. We remained warm friends until her passing. Her task was to light up the space around her so all of us could see ahead, and mine was simply to make her laugh. I continue with the work she gave me, as best I can.

WHAT TO LEARN:

Angie's life was a great gift to many people. She thought deeply about life, and combined ancient wisdom with contemporary knowledge and research. Through her teaching and writing, many of us were motivated to dig much deeper into questions of life's purpose and the nature of service. Perhaps her raw kindness was her biggest gift and lesson. How can we emulate her lovely model?

Joe Henderson, Character Shaper

Just when my life was flailing, uneasy, and more than a little ennui ridden, I found the *Shaman from Elko*.[44] This shaman was Joe Henderson, a highly acclaimed Jungian analyst. Indeed, when I met Joe, he was the last practicing analyst who'd studied directly with Carl

Jung in Zurich.

After graduating from Princeton University, Joe went to England to get his medical degree. He pursued a lovely woman from the Darwin family and married her. He became popular among the titled, literary, and dashing set, ministering to such notables as T. S. Eliot.

The Henderson ranch, where Joe grew up herding cattle, was in the hardscrabble desert outside Elko, Nevada. He loved to talk about sleeping rough during cattle drives: He had been mesmerized by the saturation of stars blinking in the heavens, which herders have found so alluring and message-bearing throughout the ages. When I met Joe, he was in his late 80s, still commuting from his home in Marin County to his Pacific Heights offices in San Francisco. Given his small face and almost delicate body, it was hard to read "cowboy." But beneath his Savile Row suits, custom shirts, and silk ties were the easy frame and movements of a born and bred rancher.

Joe was many things: scholar, healer, WASP-maven, pixie-wise man, and a terrible driver. His handsome, new, royal blue Volvo had scrapes on both sides where fenders had been used as "curb feelers." While utterly oblivious to dented fenders, he would fret about a mis-placed tomato plant in his tidy garden.

Joe took me into his practice as an exception, as I would learn later. His typical clients were senior Jungian analysts, scholars, and celebrities like artist Jackson Pollock and director George Lucas. They used Joe's therapy in their work. For example, Pollack's psychothera-peutic paintings were fashioned as part of his work with Joe, and Lucas credited Joe with helping him give *Star Wars* an archetypal resonance. Brilliant!

I was the odd specimen among these exotics. As head of CSPP (California School of Professional Psychology), a four-campus, 2,400-

student graduate school focused on the doctoral-level, I brought Joe a sense of where the overall state of psychotherapy was drifting. I was able to satisfy some of Joe's keen yearning to remain contemporary— exploring everything from psychotropic drugs to encounter groups. It was an uneven sharing, as I got the deep stuff I really needed.

W H A T   T O   L E A R N :

Joe was indifferent to age. He went on seeing clients and colleagues until he was 101. He remained eager to learn and to dive deeply into whatever his psyche hungered for. He taught many to keep learning; he was a Merlin for the middle years. He taught me that memory loss was most often a dampening of passion for learning, and that by accessing the unconscious we find our true work, our creativity, our vibrant spirit of awe and calm beyond the chaos of everyday living.

Joe taught me how to access creativity through the use of one's digits (that is, the direct method), and through meditation and dream interpretation (indirect but no less powerful). He taught many of us to find the way into the dark shadows we keep in our repression lockers, where we hide errors and lost dreams. He pressed us to turn this dark material of the unconscious into gold, just as Jung had taught him.

Joe foraged for wisdom in ancient art, native practices, and rituals. Like Jung, he was drawn to tribal healing, rain dances, and all shamanistic beliefs and practices. Always patient, he nudged me along through my writing of *The Paradox of Success*. I'm sure he overlooked my scrapes as if they were no more than "feelers" on the road to learning something deeper, and I did. One day, I brought him a dream to help me analyze. It was filled with rather graphic symbols and strange characters. He got up and moved quickly to his bookcase, which was vast, reached up, and pulled out a richly illustrated book of archetypes from the time of Mesopotamia. He flipped through the pages and showed me a rendering of my dream. From the excitement of his voice, I knew that his thrill in learning was still at work. I continue to feel that same excitement in pursuing new questions.

Noel Day, Character Shaper

Noel, a dear friend and business associate, was a wise, talented, funny, gentle slab of a man. And he was one of the first African Americans from Harlem to attend Dartmouth. I once asked him how the whole Dartmouth experience had been for him. Here's how he responded: "Football was my meal ticket, but I fell in love with nature, hiking, and canoeing. My best life advice came from my canoe coach. Here is what he told me: 'Noel, you are imposingly big and quietly smart, so you can afford to be gentle. Live life as a gentle man.'"

When I worked with Noel, he was a community organizer and consultant. He taught people how to protest nonviolently, using the same strategies he learned from the examples of Martin Luther King and Mahatma Gandhi. A gentle activist and a great friend, Noel was a true wisdom guide and a solid musician; he composed and sang songs, mostly protest or romantic ballads.

WHAT TO LEARN:

Each of us has strengths of one kind or another. Some of us are gifted athletically, some find numbers easy to play with, and some have a natural compassion for what others need. Whatever our gifts may be, they can allow us to be generous of spirit and open to the needs of others. Noel's hero (and one of mine) was the South African revolutionary leader Nelson Mandela, a man who used his personal discipline and strength to forgive his enemies and retain a generosity of soul (more on Mandela later).

When he wrote his poem, "Song of Myself," Walt Whitman, no doubt, had someone like Noel in mind: "Do I contradict myself?/ Very well, then I contradict myself,/ (I am large, I contain multitudes)."[45]

T. H. White, Wisdom Carrier

In T. H. White's lovely volume, *The Once and Future King*, depicting the education of a prince—the future King Arthur—we see how Merlin, a figure we might call a Wisdom Carrier, devises ways to make learning exciting, even magical. He also teaches young Arthur to learn from the animal world and offers corollary lessons on the virtue of humility.

The wisdom Merlin offers all of us is to understand that we can never learn it all and that being "ignorant" is a good antidote for personal egotism. Indeed, Arthur must learn humility and achieve by attempting new learning—what Buddhists call the "beginner's mind." White imagines the wizard urging the young prince on, in the following passage:

"The best thing for being sad," replied Merlyn, beginning to puff and blow, "is to learn something. That is the only thing that never fails. You may grow old and trembling in your anatomies, you may lie awake at night listening to the disorder of your veins, you may miss your only love, you may see the world about you devastated by evil lunatics, or know your honor trampled in the sewers of baser minds. There is only one thing for it then—to learn. Learn why the world wags and what wags it. That is the only thing which the mind can never exhaust, never alienate, never be tortured by, never fear or distrust, and never dream of regretting. Learning is the thing for you. Look at what a lot of things there are to learn—pure science, the only purity there is. You can learn astronomy in a lifetime, natural history in three, literature in six. And then, after you have exhausted a milliard lifetimes in biology and medicine and theocriticism and geography and history and economics— why, you can start to make a cartwheel out of the appropriate wood, or spend fifty years learning to begin to learn to beat your adversary at fencing. After that you can start again on mathematics, until it is time to learn to plough."[46]

W H A T   T O   L E A R N :

White and others make a strong case that learning is renewing, even healing.

Readings for Act II

- *How to Live: A Life of Montaigne* by Sarah Bakewell—Using her deep knowledge of Montaigne's prolific essay output, Bakewell offers the reader her formula for fashioning a good life.[47]

- *The Great Gatsby* by F. Scott Fitzgerald—An American classic tale of ambition, this novel explores what fuels an outside drive for success and what brings it to an end. The writing and the story are clear and compelling.[48]

- *The Feminine Mystique* by Betty Friedan—In her provocative and historically relevant book, Friedan details the tragic loss of women's voices and energy in society. It became a manual for the women's movement.[49]

- *Mastery: The Keys to Success and Long-Term Fulfillment* by George Leonard—In this wise treatise on learning one's way to mastery, Aikido sensei and philosopher Leonard lays out the path that mastery requires.[50] He would give support and guidance in my writing of *Leadership Aikido*.[51]

- *How to Practice* by Dalai Lama—The compelling idea of growing a spiritual life through practice is made real by this master.[52]

- *Gifts from the Sea* by Ann Morrow Lindberg—This beautifully written story reminds us of the importance and enchantment of nature's gifts and solitude.[53]

- *The Paradox of Success: When Winning at Work Means Losing at Life* by John O'Neil—By using case studies and drawing on the wisdom of others, my own book spells out steps required to find renewal in one's life.[54]

POEMS
FOR STAYING ON THE PATH

It is vital to understand what real transitions require in both preparation and recovery. Poems can help cover that ground without the ponderous phrases of philosophers and would-be gurus. We need to take all of this seriously and yet find the humor needed to survive.

Sexy Aging

Waking from a peaceful nap or snore—
How did that sexy movie end? Curious,
the things people expose themselves to,
some better left artfully covered.

How lovely, gently the pace goes.
No hurry—or is it "no problem" these days?

The sweetest peaches are now ripe.
Here, eat one—why wait?
Peaches don't really last.

Flirt outrageously—you're safe.
The best days seem short to me;
does my watch need repair?

Everywhere you look
in these X-rated times: lots of action.
Prufrock would be able
to do his manly duty.
Just watch him come and go,
eating peaches everywhere.

Old Metaphors and New

Sell-by date! Redundant! Bucket list!
Awful, demeaning words and phrases.
Who needs these cheap shots?

Not some supple yoga mama
in her sixties.
She's abloom with generous life force.
Not that elegant dancing man in his seventies,
or tireless caregivers in their eighties.

Look at cool Dave Brubeck, who played on into his 90s,
or Marion McPartland, who kept singing.

Let's have a contest for fresh metaphors.
I'll sign up.
But first, let's all dance ahead gracefully,
boogying, clowning, creating, moving.
A starter set for now.
More apt, thoughtful words to follow.

Pumping Iron

Workouts demand you glance
at your abs,
a nasty bit of the grand process of transformation.
"Hey, look at me," abs holler.
Indeed, look. Work needed.

How to distinguish wisdom from vanity?
Shakespeare got it, Lear didn't, and
Cordelia suffered for it.
Now in the land of pumping iron,
I look with vain hopes at my abs.

Progress? Sadness? Do abs give up?
Can modern science give us fresh answers?
Are ab transplants all the rage in Croatia?

Can I search web pages to get started?
Does Amazon have an ab belt I can order?
What does the AMA say?
Do their words matter?
Who knows?

Where is Oprah when I need her?
Is she focused on her abs?
I hope not.

How Dreams Show the Way

Freud said dreams were
the royal road to the unconscious.
Imagine that.
We can all take it,
a free ride.
Or is there a toll, a fee?

Perhaps all that free sex
in moist dreams
has a hidden cost
we fail to calculate,
because the mundane life
is more an alley than a road.

Royal roads spoil us and
make the bus far less erotic.
Dreams focus our awareness
of what might be,
but leave us tethered to
our tired desks.

Dreaming about dreams is the
shaman's answer.
Of course you need to smoke
the nasty pipe he offers.
He can take you into a dream of salvation,
Don't dawdle, hurry! God awaits!

Does Maturity Make Us Better Consumers?

Experience should make us better buyers,
yet when forced with a hard choice,
we buy the red one,
or we pick the one
the salesperson likes,
the cute one who cares.

We don't consume with our
left hemisphere;
we expect a rush or tingle,
a perfect rose.

How short the half-life
of a purchase.
Depreciation starts when we get home.
The trick is to get our hopes
under control,
to remember there is no consumer road
to heaven,
only warranties we will lose.

Marc Antony, who won
many a battle,
consumed what he conquered in one way or another.
Ironically, it was the Egyptian queen he won
who consumed him.

ACT III

TAKING STOCK
[AND REPROVISIONING]
··· AGE 50-65 ···

The dreaded midlife seems far less threatening after it's over. Okay, half of life is finished, but a new beginning is required and that's good news. This is a time of repentance; a time to start again. Your mojo drops and your abs simply don't behave. Large life crises loom, especially regarding use of time. How much time is needed to recover lost abs? The second half of life is to be the creative half. Research shows that creativity emanates from a different part of the brain than we generally use. Neuroscience can pinpoint where music resides and how different neurons get triggered when creating it. British neurologist Oliver Sacks was totally absorbed with this puzzle of music storage because he had seen people with advanced Alzheimer's (including his mother), who could recall music when they had lost other functionality.[55]

Through the transition process, there is no substitute for a strong guide—someone who has been down that road. My mentor, John Gardner, filled that role for me and for others. My first true appreciation of the need to "repot" came from him.

What are some early indications of the need for renewal?

- Routines and ennui that feel like a heavy slog
- A tendency to listen to the same people on similar themes
- Clinging to certain beliefs and resisting challenging them
- Becoming risk averse
- Daydreaming about various exploits never taken

Character Shapers and Wisdom Carriers

Gun and Tom Denhart, Character Shapers

I met this dynamic couple at a Social Venture Network (SVN) meeting in Santa Barbara. I had just finished a talk on leadership and values, and they waited patiently until others left so they could talk with me. Gun, a young Swedish-American woman, was radiant: Blonde and blue-eyed, she could have been a catalog model (which she was). Tom, a big, warm, American guy, was a model of the casual but highly successful businessman (which he was).

Over coffee, Gun and Tom told me the story of how they had started a catalog clothing company in their garage in Connecticut. Originally, they had sold bold-colored, durable, kids' clothes from Sweden. Now they were mailing out a thicker catalog, which offered more lines including some for women. The enterprise was growing fast, and customer satisfaction was unusually high. Their brand, Hanna Andersson, was achieving almost cult-like popularity, especially among young parents.

I discovered that the Denharts had come to my SVN talk with a purpose, when Tom gently asked, "Could you come visit us in our new building in Portland? We need help on leadership, governance, and strategy." It was easy to say, "Yes," to this charming, smart, and remarkably kind couple. Our friendship and work together grew over many years. I helped them hit growth and profit targets year after year, as well as create a solid board and an amazing leadership team. The company and the couple grew in fame—a Swedish-American success story.

When Tom was diagnosed with cancer, my role expanded, and we began to think about the challenges of Act IV for them and for the company. Gun, still young and vital, gradually assumed more and more responsibility, and I urged her to bring on a chief executive officer, which she did. As their children grew up, family affairs became more complex. I finally urged the family to bring in an investment advisor, Jean-Michele Valette, who magically found the perfect buyer for the company.

Later, after Tom had passed, my rich friendship with Gun continued. She stays with us when she's in the Bay Area or attending The Good Life Seminar. My wife Pat and I have taken some wonderful trips with Gun, including to Patagonia and Africa. Our love for Gun and her family continues to expand.

WHAT TO LEARN:

There's magic in relationships, and that magic changes again and again. It may start in one place and wind up in a different one. It's the damnedest, most confounding process, and it calls upon our best and highest virtues including gratitude and compassion. Despite the difficulties, I wouldn't have it any other way. It makes for a grand experience, with lasting benefits.

Pat O'Neil, Character Shaper

When I ran into Pat on Union Street in San Francisco (after not having seen her for quite some time) I was returning to my office with a woman at my side. Our first misunderstanding came right then: Pat assumed my companion was someone of interest to me, when in fact I had just given that woman her walking papers. I immediately invited Pat to come to my office for a cup of tea and cleared that up!

I had always admired Pat, and had enjoyed her company since we first met, when I was serving in the Air Force with her then-husband Barry. Pat is beautiful, razor-sharp, funny, holds deep-abiding values, and has lots of style. After catching up, dating began. But as veterans of broken marriages who were both living full, enjoyable lives, we felt no compulsion to rush into marriage.

It's lovely to be head-over-heels in love, even in Act III of one's life—perhaps especially then. We were certainly compatible; there was mutual stimulation; and we both enjoyed wonderful learning adventures. Pat continued her graduate studies and was awarded two masters' degrees: one in Psychology and the other in Theology. I continued to run the CSPP graduate school and began writing books and giving talks and seminars on leadership.

Pat and I continue to enjoy traveling together, whether for business or adventure, and our mutual love of art and music adds a delightful overlay to our various work and pleasure junkets. Pat is also a superb hostess and cook, which helps to keep our social life robust.

A relationship is difficult to capture in greeting card style without sounding trite or even smug. Like all life partners, we enjoy the work of family as well as its ample rewards. Should a grandchild suffer, we feel the kind of pain and frustration that is both universal and deeply personal.

One of the biggest gifts is having our family all around us, as well as friends who give us equal measures of succor and challenge. Pat remains my constant loving, learning partner in all aspects of life. What a gift.

WHAT TO LEARN:

The list of things I learn from my special partner and teacher is long and elaborate. One recurring lesson is how to enjoy the smallest bits of life while pushing, reaching, and even occasionally touching the larger aspects of it. The key is to wander deeply into each day with gentle probes. Cut out cynicism—it serves no one. Love daringly, freely, without expectations. Keep giggling.

|||||||||||||||||||||||||||||||||||||||||||||||||||||||||||||||||||||||||||||||||||||||||||||||||||||||||||||||||||||||||||||||||||||||||||||||||||||||||||||||||||||||||||||

Rob Johnson, Character Shaper

There are bright people, and then there is Rob. The words "incendiary" and "deep" come close to describing his mind. We first met in Davos, Switzerland in 1996, following a seminar I had just moderated. He had read my book, *The Paradox of Success*, on a flight from New York to Beijing; called his wife Bonnie in Greenwich, Connecticut; and requested to meet with me in Davos. I said, "Yes."

When you first meet Rob, there is a warm intensity surrounding him as he lays out his thoughts and needs and what connects them to you. There's nothing coy about him; only straightforward facts and solid reasoning that connects and envelops you. Rob and Bonnie had a mission: Their very large financial success had come quickly, and they felt ill prepared for it, so they were seeking the skills to cope with their new status.

In 1992, as managing director at Soros Funds, Rob, with a small team, had pulled off a raid on the British Pound on what became known as "Black Wednesday" in the U.K. This coup and others brought a level of wealth and notoriety Rob knew he was not psychologically ready to handle. As he'd read in *Paradox*, he became increasingly aware of a dark shadow that massive wealth casts, which must be transformed to light or great harm can follow.

We became instant learning partners and have remained so (he has attended The Good Life Seminar, eager and ready to learn and teach). Though he continues to be media-shy, Rob works to break down today's economic theories by creating fresh approaches that depart from those set by the academic cartel. Rob, like other independent-minded people, wants to bring wisdom forward and, like Montaigne, make it available and useful for everyone.

WHAT TO LEARN:

We must continue to challenge orthodoxy and groupthink wherever we find it. Rob models the life of a true autodidact, always digging deeper and pushing aside worn-out concepts and theories. Start by searching inside: What do I know and what do I need to learn? What new learning partners can I work with? How can I increase intensity of thought and throw out ennui and tedium? As Dylan Thomas urges, we all need to "rage against the dying of the light" and "not go gentle into that good night."[56]

Jeremy Tarcher, Character Shaper

Jeremy Tarcher was a publisher who loved not only books but also learning and the good life—a wise man. Working with him on *The Paradox of Success* in 1974 was like taking an advanced tutorial on writing and thinking. He could easily have been an Oxford Don. He made his authors work very hard; sweat was a necessary byproduct of an editing session.

The topic of *Paradox* is the ensuing psychological and spiritual dangers following hyper-success—that is, too much success, too soon. Jeremy saw this in his own world of publishing in New York, and in the entertainment world that his wife, Shari Lewis, inhabited in Hollywood as a highly successful host and puppeteer on her television show, *Lamb Chop's Play Along*.

Jeremy and Shari were an extremely attractive and well-matched couple—not flashy, but they stood out. For a new writer like me, they were mesmerizing in their sophistication and charm. They were alike in temperament and curiosity and even in size and appearance. Both were small and well formed. She had big, black, cheerful eyes, and he could have been an academic Steve McQueen.

Jeremy and his chief editor, Connie Sweig, both took a personal interest in my book. They were well versed in psychology and had seen the devastating results of hubris, which certainly was endemic to the worlds of power and prancing they occupied. Jeremy's sister, Judith Krantz, a best-selling romance novelist, drew heavily from the actual lives of the rich and famous in writing her books.

What pleased yet intimidated me most was the relentless pressure Jeremy applied in his efforts to improve the manuscript. He had been referred to me by Dick Gunther, a mutual friend whom we both admired. Thus, I had referral "creds." But it was the subject matter and the stories that made Jeremy proclaim, "*Paradox* will be a big book—an evergreen book." Seemed cool to me.

As a good product of St. John's College, Jeremy was well read and curious, the perfect preparation for a publisher. We first met in his Beverly Hills office, and quickly began intense work on every aspect of the book. He loved to edit and would arrive at my house with red ink-slashed pages of my precious text. He seemed addicted to continuously improving everything—from stories and case studies to punctuation.

When I got Jeremy to tell me about his own life, I began to understand the passion behind his interest in the book itself. Money had been a very taboo topic in his house. He mentioned that his mother had once said, "I would rather have you see me on the toilet than talk about money."

As tough-minded and tenacious as he was, Jeremy could also be quite generous and kind. He wanted to prepare me for the smallish and fragile spate of fame the book would bring. And he was there to support me as my 60 seconds of recognition came. When he sold his imprint and backlist to Penguin, he made sure I was well attended to. He helped me with my next book, *Seasons of Grace*, which I co-authored with Alan Jones and Diana Landau. Jeremy was a lovely, generous man.

WHAT TO LEARN:

Our characters are shaped by events, changes, and new challenges that come along. We might try thinking of this process as the perturbation of a growing system. If our natural inclination is to keep life the same—as is true for so many of us—we need a perturbator like Jeremy to give us a disturbing nudge that will prompt us to learn something new at the right time. Try it. You have everything to lose—and lots of new learning to gain.

Nelson Mandela, Wisdom Carrier: What a Great Leader Looks Like

We all need learning guides—some who will prod us and others who will cheer us on. We also need people we can admire and who can teach us by their life example—by what they say and what they do. I found that role model in Nelson Mandela.

Because of his unusual gifts and the challenges that confronted him, Nelson Mandela had to learn, again and again, the powerful, redemptive lessons of life. Standing in the Kongress Center at the Davos World Economic Forum in 1998, I witnessed an unprecedented response to a world leader. As Mandela entered the room, 2,500 other world leaders were on their feet applauding wildly, and as he loped across the stage, the volume increased, and the tears flowed. Later I would meet him, and he would implore me, "Come to South Africa, we need you." I said, "Of course." Little did I know he meant for me to run a leadership development program there.

What was so special about Mandela? What did he release in each of us? What connections were made, unbidden but deep? This was more than celebrity, although that was present. His buttoned-up casual shirt and the wide, generous smile were familiar to us; we knew him, and we admired his heroic story. And here he was in his fourth act of life, standing humbly before us.

The words "discipline" and "learning" came up frequently in my interviews with leaders who knew Mandela. They were also invoked by his former prison guard, who became a tour guide at the Robben Island prison museum and showed us Mandela's meager possessions that had been saved in his old cell. He spoke with clear reverence for the man's discipline, training regimens, reading, and discourse. Mandela's friends had smuggled reading and writing materials to him while the white guards had turned their backs. He carried on correspondence through visitors who acted as couriers. Mandela studied and emulated role models: Perhaps Gandhi and Martin Luther King had the greatest influence on him—through them, he found inspiration in the famed Russian writer Leo Tolstoy who had been enthralled by the ascetic beliefs of various religious leaders. Mandela's autodidactic discipline allowed him to forge his own sacred documents on the role of government and democratic processes.

The man who was to be my advisor-escort for the leadership program met me at the Johannesburg Airport, a massive, confusing place. Like a character from one of director Woody Allen's comedies, I was struggling to get my bags off the carousel when a very tall, thin, simply dressed man carrying a staff appeared at my side and said, "Are you O'Neil?" I acknowledged that I was, and he introduced himself as Mayo. "I am here to watch over you," he said calmly and gently. He was Mandela's godson and my minder-advisor-friend for the duration of my stay.

With Mayo in charge, we quickly had the bags stowed in the back of a waiting Range Rover, and we headed for the bush. Besides being Mandela's godson, Mayo was a professor of philosophy who had been educated in the old USSR and in the USA, at Syracuse University. Mayo had a blend of gifts: gentle strength, warming curiosity, and political astuteness.

Over the next several days, at a very isolated inn and conference center, Mayo remained at my side. "The bush and this meeting are filled with all types of snakes," he cautioned, "and since you appear to be the kind of person who might step on a snake, I will warn you." He was truly a godsend.

From his studies of Abraham Lincoln, Mandela had learned the virtues of including highly skilled and knowledgeable former rivals in his Cabinet, so our leadership-development group included former highly placed Afrikaners, as well as bright but inexperienced ANC members. All were hard working and, as Mayo described them, "screened for learning capacity and curiosity."

Representing the extremes were a white male logistics expert who had served under President de Klerk, and a black female physician who had been "approved" by ANC leaders to run social services. By the end of our time in the bush, these two had become learning partners and led the exercise in creating the new mission statement for South Africa's future.

Each day after our "avoiding-snakes" walk, Mayo would call Mandela and brief him on our progress. The following day, I would receive some encouragement or suggestions and that was it. One of Mandela's main objectives was to make sure this group became a learning team that would spread a new culture of innovation and learning across the government.

A huge bonus was the humor that surfaced as the stress began to feel unbearable. We found our class clowns and they were us. Each of us was from a vastly different background and in a different stage of life. Yet we found creativity and joy in meeting Mandela's initiatives in the middle of the snake-filled bush.

WHAT TO LEARN:

Integrity was the key to all Mandela power. He was very direct, well informed, humble, and persuasive. Leaders need those qualities. The power of intense focus is critical for both learning and teaching. Discipline had kept Mandela alive as, day by day, he had prayed and dug deeply into his inner resources to survive deprivation of the worst kind.

Readings for Act III

- *Self-Renewal* by John Gardner—In this profound book, Gardner offers remedies for learning stagnation. He tells why we need to "repot" on a thoughtfully planned basis.[57]

- *Transitions* by Bill Bridges—Bridges offers advice on the proper way to view transitions. He uses strong visual images of crossing a river in conveying the decisions that life changes require.[58]

- *Painting as a Pastime* by Sir Winston Churchill—This beautiful little book describes the author's own transition from lost power to forced retirement and newfound creativity.[59]

- *Churchill's Black Dog, Kafka's Mice, and Other Phenomena of the Human Mind* by Anthony Storr—Storr offers a stunning review of what creativity can do to heal damaged psyches.[60]

- *Drawing on the Right Side of the Brain* by Betty Edwards—For those of us seeking to upgrade our creative gifts, Edwards truly offers help. She leads the reader through the thicket that doing creative work often presents.[61]

- *Rules for Aging: A Wry and Witty Guide to Life* by Roger Rosenblatt—This is the book that prompted me to write my own guide. Rosenblatt approaches aging with wisdom that's carefully layered with gentle humor.[62]

POEMS
FOR RENEWAL

What Our Words Tell Us

There are either too many words or
none at all.
Often we have a surfeit that
seem strangely recycled.
Note how words can go all shy and hide.

Note how words can dance and dart about,
searching for relevance,
while we curse senior moments or that last drink.
When did words refuse to march in a tidy line?

Some zig, others zag, or merely wander off.
We dance around the voids
as if we'd planned to use some odd construction,
like Gaudí venturing into cathedral design,
the odd and irregular posing as flashes of genius.
Yet who dares call us out, since we all know
about the curious ways of the avant garde?

Life's Inventory

After we order our usual
chai latte with soy,
a full-body inventory can begin.
First the knees,
then the back
and other assorted parts.

It's strange how these visits work—
not as a full anatomy course
or an annual physical,
but more a show of empathy,
a compassion jag
that never fails to heal our psyches.

Imagine having coffee with Freud,
a devoted hypochondriac.
Were the teeth and the digestion
at the top of his list,
or was it dark sleeping issues,
X-rated dreams?

My latte-drinking friend has
old sports injuries—
a lot less erotic,
but no less important.
So we do our body scans
and sip away.

Superannuated Heroes

Jung stated that
the first half of life
is prep for the second,
and the second is to be
the creative half.

What delicious words to fondle, sleep with.
Pablo Casals knew this and kept noodling,
squeezing and caressing his man-sized instrument
with gnarly digits.

No one told Grandma Moses
she was too old
to paint gay, childish scenes
of familiar places.

Ludwig couldn't hear, poor guy.
"Ludwig, stop! You're deaf!"
But he kept on composing and
we keep on listening.
Agatha Christie kept her mysteries coming, plus
plays and poems and short stories.
And we kept reading,
No one bothered to tell her,
"After Poirot, give it up,"
and thankfully, she wrote on.

Work Ahead

So the old bull says to the young one:
"Work can be frantic, hard rushed,
with too many cows needing our help."
Can our fall days of dazzling hues
be thoughtfully stretched with right work?

Churchill worked past his prime;
even Picasso stayed productive with his young-bull style.
Both were randy in their ambitious ways.
How did Georgia O'Keeffe fight ennui?
Did her young companions help?
Florence Nightingale invented modern nursing
in her second phase of life;

even from bed she hectored generals and admirals,
asking that they keep things clean,
"For health's sake."
So lives were saved and spirits raised.

Because genius has no sell-by date,
our work will begin promptly after nap.
We'll strap on our spurs and go watch some cows.
Work on!

Listen Up and Live

There's a huge premium on listening:
it's a scarce resource.
People pay therapists outrageous
hourly fees to be heard.
Charlie Brown was a sucker,
but therapy he got.

A famous ad man named Ogilvy
won a client because
he was such a good listener.
Later he confessed, "I couldn't speak
because I was too drunk."

I've heard that ardent listening
is an aphrodisiac.
An earnest friend took a course
on active listening.
He had his sights set on a buxom talker;
she went on and on while he slept.

As people age, they have a choice:
to talk or listen.
Churchill picked talk,
so his wife chose travel.
Any road worked for her
to escape Winnie's speeches,
addressing Parliament
from his bathtub.

Getting Help for Success

Carl Jung, in his Swiss-like way,
was not given to gushing.
To people arriving,
he would say, enthusiastically,
"I hear you have had success;
I hope it hasn't hurt you too much."

So as we move ahead seeking
dubious fame and fortune,
let's pause quietly, okay?
Do we have the right map?
Are we well prepared? Indeed,
what happens if we succeed?

A very rich guy came to visit Jung,
worried that he'd made a mistake.
Had he lived his life all wrong?
Could there be a treatment for
his disease of success, or was it fatal?
Jung assured him he would survive.

He had tried to skip the stages of growth
and thought money would be a fast-pass.
He'd missed empathy, love,
and childlike joy on his way to success,
and now he felt deep pain
and had to start again.

Alaskan Spiritual Moments

How lucky we are to have sublime moments,
unexpected revelations.
Not too many to blunt the impact of surprise—
just ones that shout:
"Look! I have a message for you!"

I saw a happy porpoise today,
surfing our boat's wake.
Why are these ancient messengers always grinning?
What's behind their secret joy, their Dalai Lama smile?

Ancient mariners were terrified of bad omens,
and properly so, as a red sky could deliver death—
just ask Odysseus.
Can a skimming porpoise bring salvation?

Who better, you ask, to send the right message?
It's up to us to be the ones
who translate messages from little squirmy cetaceans
into hope.

Will we allow these intrepid divine ones
to bring us unbidden joy? Or do we have
bigger fish to fry?

Words, Words, Words

Words, words, words. Do they keep me alive?
Sentences grow more elaborate
as I strain to tell a story just right.
Conjunctions have become my most trusted allies,

Like tiny defibrillators kicking the heart awake.
An *and* here or a *but* there
presses my sentences on and on.
How will I know when my words
collapse into prattle?

Will someone's expression read
Stop, you bore me,
or will I merely fall into a
heap of words, words, words?
Or may I find myself talked into a box seat
as a listener in Dante's hell?

Was Sartre right that hell is here
in the form of others' words,
or will silence fall healingly around me?
Let's tiptoe on and find out.

My Rapper Phase

Tried rapping this morning but got delayed.
Special *K* intervened, as food trumped art again.

My rap efforts have an edge,
a spot of anger.
Always the same anger, like bad driving.

Got the Prius all pimped out, big bass, Dolby thumping.
Big thumps equal big balls—right?
All like *Yo, whatsupbro?*
Thump thump thump!

People seem to notice—are they admiring?
Maybe they're listening for a fetching melody.
It's there!
Only you old folks just can't hear it.
Like a dog whistle can't
fetch squirrels
but does give 'em migraines.

Yelled out my new rap handle
to my hearing-challenged friend:
"Yo! Call me 3 Bits, bitch!"

He fainted.

ACT IV

CURIOSER AND CURIOUSER
[GOING DEEPER INTO LIFE]
··· AGE 65-80 ···

As we proceed through the fourth act, and inevitably begin to confront our own mortality, one pressing question is "What's it all about?" Each person must make a choice about what truly matters: Is it the beauty seen, felt, and perhaps created? Is it love and truth? Are these the virtues and metrics of a good Act IV?

A friend once recounted his father's deathbed scene to me: Noticing his father clutching a piece of paper with writing on it, the son asked, "What's on the paper?" Through clenched teeth, his father answered, "A list of all the bastards I hate. Hope I didn't miss anyone."

One of my favorite stories is of two men at the funeral of a wealthy friend. One man inquires, "How much did he leave?" Without pause, the other man answers, "All of it."

My friend, Alan Jones, formerly Dean of Grace Cathedral in San Francisco, told me about "show funerals." Such a planned social event provides the public with a spectacle that display the family's wealth. In researching *Seasons of Grace*, the book I wrote with Alan, we sought out beautiful rituals used to celebrate the winter season. The theme for many of them was gratitude. The idea of embracing the lovely aspects of life with which we've fallen in love—small critters like birds and other wildlife, music, and art—seems to be the essence of a good Act IV.

In the penultimate act of life's drama, the stage begins to fill with characters: some new, others familiar; some fresh and young, others scarred and listing. Memories of those who've passed drop in and out. They appear in various forms and guises. Each play delivers new roles that add to the larger, unfolding life story.

Let's start with our children and their unique contributions. The one who rebelled and kept you on tenterhooks becomes a rock. The shy one becomes animated, fun to be around, a family scribe. And the stubborn, headstrong little girl is now comforting, empathetic, and kind. They turn out to be the companions, guides, and loving partners you need.

Others entering stage left (it was always "left," in our family) are assorted characters with various roles, from jesters to philosophers. Luckily, in my case, they're upbeat and looking for laughs, as well as for insights. Some are bawdy, even outrageous. Who cares? We have the freedom to put away our inhibitions. "Fart when you want!" is the sign above the entry. I suspect the play's director (me, in this case) has exercised considerable bias in cast selection. Why not? Let's ask ourselves, "Why would we cast dour, grumpy, narrow-minded individuals in our precious play?" I certainly wouldn't! I want my final act to be populated by actors with a keen wit, who are reflective and still seeking—even adventuresome.

I had the opportunity to write a chapter for a book called *80 Things to Do When You Turn 80*, edited by Mark Chimsky.[63] I believe it captures some of the freedom one can enjoy in Act IV, yet my in-house editor and best friend claims I missed a good chance to discuss the role of lovemaking. I feigned shyness and decided to leave that to the readers' imaginations. However, I did do some research, googling "aging" and "sex" and "Kinsey Report," but the search results returned only porn. There you have it.

Beware of taking on interesting and innocent-looking projects in Act IV. For example, last summer I began to write poems as a diversion from a badly stuck seven-year writing project. My book topic, "the future of learning," had seemed too big and dynamic; e-learning was changing its rules and players weekly; I was flummoxed by the sheer scale of it. So, I decided to write a few poems. What harm? I didn't even bother adding the task to my "to do" list. No big deal, right? Before long—40 poems later and counting—the exercise compellingly morphed into components for a different book (this one).

So here I am—a healthy and experienced player with a brilliant wife, incredible children, and delightful grandchildren—but I still haven't learned how to stay on task. And now I found myself like tired, aging Odysseus heading home from Troy with sirens beckoning him off course.

Recognizing the Muse

In the middle muddle of my life, Merlin appeared to me in the form of John Gardner, a leadership maven who taught me how to respect my learning compulsions. Another actor, Joe Henderson, a Jungian analyst, taught me how creative learning can help in healing. My wife, Pat, showed up to guide and support me.

Winston Churchill, another learning hero, wrote about how creativity changed the second half of his life. Once he was out of government (and power), Churchill retreated to Chartwell, his country estate. In his lovely book, *Painting as a Pastime*, he describes the transition as, "Like a sea beast hoisted from the depths—my veins threatening to burst from the lack of pressure—it was then the muse of painting came to my rescue."[64]

In my case, writing became the muse. But in order to balance all the other competing, glittering prospects, I established some rules of engagement and practices that you, too, might consider taking up:

- **Make Lists**—When you enter Act IV, it's important to have lots of lists: to-do's, should-haves, apologies, and big ideas. Any damned fool can make a to-do list, but at 80 years old, it should become an art. When you're younger, you can, for example, write the word "gym" on your calendar, and no additional details are needed. At 80, your list should include everything you'll need to take along to the gym, such as: a book to read on the bike, or earbuds with which to watch TV or listen to an inspirational podcast (designate which one). And don't forget Ace bandages and water, lots of water!

- **Hang Out with Young People**—The beauties of the art of mentoring are spelled out in Ricardo Levy's book, *Letters to a Young Entrepreneur*.[65] Find younger people who will become learning partners, including your children and grandchildren. Be sure to include new people and make your list (yet another list!) diverse. It's amazing how many young people will find your experience and life lessons valuable. But this will be the case only if your stories are carefully curated to be of value to them. Reminiscences, homilies, and moral tales can be heavy, boring, and devoid of learning value for your partners. Also, I'd advise you to resist trying out your new rap music on them, as good as it might be. I did that, and I got guffaws in return.

- **Create a Learning Plan**—If you want to fashion a bucket list, that's okay, but only if it's filled with learning journeys. Learning should be exciting, adventurous, and deeply satisfying, not just another trip with too much food and booze. There are several new learning curves for you to consider, with lists to match. What dreams and ambitions have you set aside that might be revisited? Who do you admire and want to learn from—whether alive or dead? (Yes, dead is not a problem. In fact, I've had Montaigne as a learning partner for years, although I'm not sure he got much out of it.) Dig deep inside, perhaps learning to meditate so you can reclaim those outrageous aspirations you once put aside as unrealistic. Perhaps your next learning challenge can be an interior one. Helen Luke, in a powerful book called *Old Age*, tells of Odysseus finally returning home from his dramatic adventures only to start a new journey.[66] Luke, a Jungian, insists that the weary warrior must now go inside and discover who he really is. So must we all.

- **Work Out**—Evidence mounts that good physical workouts are needed for mental health. It seems that a functioning cortex needs oxygen. Too simplistic? Try it. Besides, it makes you feel good, and while your abs might feel sore, they may look better (at least when you hold your breath). There are several things to be said for workouts aside from feeling righteous: Put on a headset and you can escape from all life's noise and demands (or not, depending on what you tune into). Skip the headset and you can make new friends who are buff (or not, depending on how intimidated you feel), Some even claim workout clothes are hip, so you can sport them all day long, even if they're sweat-stained (or not, depending on just how stylin' you want to be).

- **Practice Gratitude**—The ancient Greek statesman, Cicero, said, "Gratitude is not only the greatest of virtues, but the parent of all the others."[67] If you're still motoring, be grateful. Be grateful for friends and family, freedom, opportunities, beauty, sunshine, small flowers, animals, poems, mighty trees. Create rituals of gratitude. My personal favorite is the gratitude walk suggested by Zen Master Thich Nhat Hanh, who advised, "Each mindful breath, each mindful step, reminds us that we are alive on this beautiful planet. We don't need anything else. It is wonderful enough just to be alive, to breathe in, and to make one step. We have arrived at where real life is available— the present moment."[68] I suggest you try it today.

When Pete Thigpen and I moderated The Good Life Seminar, we started with a gratitude walk. It cleared the mind and readied the soul for learning. All of The Good Life Seminar alumni are learning partners. Lucky us. As I fashion new books, I crave and receive ideas, research, and critiques from all of my trusted learning partners, of all ages. I am so grateful.

Curiouser and Curiouser Reflections

Fortunate indeed are those who enter Act IV with couples as friends and learning partners. Alas many, in my case, have become more intermittently available as various ailments and daunting distances keep us separated. Of course, we visit electronically, but digital hugs just ain't the same. We have lovely survivors to keep up with and even travel with occasionally; we relished our trips to Africa and Patagonia with our dear friend Gun Denhart.

It's important to remember that it takes seasoning to bring a steak to perfection. Indeed, salt may be invaluable for much of life's flavoring. I notice, during the fourth act, that eating and planning and talking about good food and wine can swell in its contribution to "a good life" (along with art, music, and books, of course).

As the fourth act progresses, each of us drops (or perhaps "misplaces" is a more gracious word) bits and pieces of capability. The long checklist (not unlike one for getting a 747 off the ground) includes: walking, hearing, seeing, remembering, sleeping, and digesting. All Act IV conversations may contain status reports on these and other conditions.

Whoever coined the phrase "senior moments" contributed an acceptable way to describe memory loss. For some, a new phrase may be needed, as these moments extend into hours. We must await science's remedies. But in the meantime, patience and empathy are truly needed to make Act IV graceful.

Character Shapers and Wisdom Carriers

Pete Thigpen, Character Shaper

It's no exaggeration to say that one of the stars of my fourth act was Pete Thigpen, co-moderator of The Good Life Seminar. Pete passed this year, and I gave up the seminar. We pushed each other to find fresh material focused on big themes. Lately, our attention had been on character building (or shaping). We reached out to wise people and borrowed shamelessly. We were especially indebted to The Good Life Seminar alumni, who offered great suggestions for themes, readings, and music. We'd even used their writings, like those we found in the book *Cut These Words into My Stone* by Michael Wolfe.[69]

Pete and I learned the seminar business at events like the Davos World Economic Forum and at places like the Aspen Institute. We tried to emulate the fine, probing style of the Aspen Executive Leadership Seminar by using great sources, often combining the wisdom of the ancients, like Plato and Aristotle, with more modern material. But the seminarians themselves ultimately generated the most intriguing insights. When we applied their own diverse experiences and backgrounds to a topic, all sorts of magic happened. For example, when we looked at how Montaigne had absorbed and used the Epicureans' theories of good living in his amazing life, the life experience of each seminarian brought the search for good living into personal focus.

Pete was a true overachiever. An athlete at Stanford, a Marine Corps carrier-based radioman, and President of Levi Strauss, Europe, Pete's resume looked like an American heroic tale. But what lay below his achievements was a rich and hungry mind. He searched for sources with a scholar's appetite for what's best. And he relished edgy discussions. Pete was an Act IV gym rat for the mind, as well as the body.

Lucky are the students at UC Berkeley and Stanford business schools who had Pete teach them Ethics. For these hyper-ambitious, millennial entrepreneurs, he provided real-life conundrums and cautionary tales.

WHAT TO LEARN:

The first thing Pete offered was a partnership in various learning expeditions. In Act III, we both gave up big physical challenges (Pete had been a triathlete). I had shed the ambition of youth and my yearning for endless achievement to turn to work on developing a deeply satisfying gratitude for new moral and intellectual tests of character. The truly fortunate become part of a learning community or create one, as Pete and I did with The Good Life Seminar.

Dick and Lois Gunther, Character Shapers

The hideous and shameful Vietnam War brought horrific suffering and waste that still lingers in the lives of its veterans and their families. For me, the only saving remnants were remarkable friendships forged with fellow antiwar activists. So, let me pay homage to the Gunthers.

When I met Dick and Lois, they were living in Beverly Hills. We were in their hot tub, armed with glasses of white wine, and I was a tad uneasy with the setting. But I had been to Esalen Institute in Big Sur (as had they), so I put on my cool, been-here-before act. They immediately put me at ease, and a lifelong conversation got underway.

From this curious beginning, we began a 35-year friendship. Pat and I were married in the Gunthers' lovely Santa Barbara beach house. For a long while, Dick and I flailed away at politics of one form or another. But the real bond was our range of interests: in art, movies, and books, in addition to politics. To this day, Pat regularly joins Dick and Lois in working on *The New York Times* crossword puzzles. Perhaps our richest times have been spent traveling, taking bike trips to exotic places, or enjoying long weekends together in Santa Barbara, playing vigorous games of tennis.

Now, the more strenuous activity has been cut way back, what with all the complaints from our hips and backs. Over the years, we've been through many losses, hurts, and setbacks, but today our great joy is in celebrating family and friends and the satisfactions that come from the realm of the mind and spirit. The Gunthers are great models of wisdom, generosity, grit, and love.

WHAT TO LEARN:

Act IV is a testing ground for friendship. The inevitable losses and pain can serve as a means of deepening the important stuff: love, tenderness, and humor. Far from just swapping pain stories, the search for new meanings and funny anecdotes grows more valuable. Gone is much of the competitiveness, and in its place comes caring, holding, and sharing.

Chuck and Diane Frankel, Character Shapers

There are friendships that do more than simply endure. In author William Faulkner's words, "They prevail."[70] In Act IV, a well-worn and gracious friendship is a much-prized gift. You can find solace in a well-lived friendship and, if truly fortunate, also the humor and intellectual challenges that keep life lubricated.

In Act IV, there are always issues of lubrication—especially in the knees and hips of wannabe jocks. With Chuck, a true stoic, unless something is really falling apart, there is not much limb discussion. We know each other's passions for learning, and for acting, when possible. For Chuck and his astonishing wife Diane, art, politics, family, and extraordinary travel adventures provide timely mental grease.

When I met Chuck, he was a senior aide to then-Senator Thomas Kuchel of California. He had grown up in Chicago, then went to college and business school at Harvard. He described himself as a "curious conservative." Spending time in the Peace Corps and working with a California liberal-leaning Republican Senator caused him to begin moving left, as prominent Republicans like Barry Goldwater, Richard Nixon, and Ronald Reagan moved right. Chuck bravely ran for a seat in the California State Assembly, in a notoriously liberal San Francisco district. He lost. But his good humor helped him to keep going.

Diane is a serious Democrat, so it's certain that dinner conversation and pillow talk facilitated Chuck's shift toward more liberal views. Also, an early tour in the Peace Corps in Botswana was a major influence on their interests in art and the Africans' struggle to find their post-Colonial bearings.

WHAT TO LEARN:

Chuck and Diane have lots of friends, many going way back. The reason for this is their fierce appetite to keep up their learning adventures. Sometimes that takes the form of lectures or discussion groups in the arts, politics, and science. They both like challenges, whether in new venues or in old stomping grounds like Africa, with new interests. It's always a delight to be with them, and I come away fresher and wiser. We all need friends who provide perspective on your life through the lens of continuous learning. Chuck and Diane opened me up to a larger world view, especially of Africa and art. Their enthusiasm for learning adventures quickens my own curiosity and sense of a larger world.

||||||||||||||||||||||||||||||||||||||||||||||||||||||||||||||||||||||||||||||||||||||||||||||||||||||||||||||||||||||||||||||||||||||||||||||||||||||

The Bury Family, Character Shapers

When Tony Bury comes after you, don't resist. He brings his whole family and they surround you with their humor and wisdom. Tony became a young client when he read *The Paradox of Success* and saw himself. He invited me to London, where I discovered the Bury magic.

Tony was a young man who had launched a remarkable collection of start-ups, scattered around the Middle East. Most of them were in the oil and gas sector. Like Tony, his brother, Martin, was also a business mover, helping guide the fortunes of a conglomerate of families, originally from Damascus.

The two brothers are still very close and support one another personally, as learning partners, and in business. Their father had been in the Royal Air Force, retiring as a successful executive in the aerospace industry. Anne, a Danish beauty, had become Tony's wife and was the mother of their daughter, Kat, who lives in Nairobi, Kenya.

The first thing I learned from Tony and his family was the virtue of taking on new challenges, physically and intellectually. As we worked to reduce the size of Tony's business holdings, we began to add new learning curves. Following the Jungian idea of the second half of life as the creative half, Tony took on a major role with the board of his former school, Prior Park College, and began to help them develop a new campus in Gibraltar. He also helped develop and grow The Good Life Seminar, both in Bath, England and in Sausalito, California. He began to add to his liberal arts education by reading poetry and the great books. For a while, he studied the harp. Following his heart and his head, Tony established a family foundation, called Mowgli Mentoring, to support young entrepreneurs in MENA (Middle East and Northern Africa). Now run by his daughter Kat, networks of mentors assist the next generation of leaders in their troubled part of the world.

WHAT TO LEARN:

The fact that someone like Tony relishes business, particularly in MENA (he was born in Zimbabwe) doesn't diminish his passion for learning in new realms. Recently, he planned an intense study tour of Japan, especially the cultural and spiritual aspects of this enchanting culture. Again, Tony turned to his brother Martin to join him in an eclectic and immersive tour that ranged from meditation to watching World Cup rugby. They are naturally curious, so they left their itinerary open for fresh experiences. My hope is that Tony and his family keep learning and teaching and continue to spread their special brand of curiosity around a needy world.

Michael Lerner and Rachel Naomi Remen, Character Shapers

When Michael Lerner started Commonweal Institute in Bolinas, California, he was interested in topics ranging from children's health to death and dying. His curiosity was wide and vivid. His brilliance, fecundity, and autodidactic reach was recognized by the MacArthur Foundation, and he was given a MacArthur Fellowship, a.k.a. a "Genius Grant."

Michael is a generous friend, sharing his knowledge with many of us, while prompting us to push further and dig deeper. In 1990, he and Rachel Remen, a clinical professor at UC Medical Center and author of splendid books on healing including the highly popular *Kitchen Table Wisdom*,[71] decided to open a program called the Cancer Help Center.

I have referred people to the program, and for those who have taken advantage of it, the results have been profoundly important in their attempts to navigate the complexity of decision-making in the face of illness, while living life as fully as possible. My friends and character shapers Tom and Gun Denhart were guided and buoyed by their stay at the center during Tom's fight with cancer.

Character shapers often appeal to our yearning for more knowledge. They spot our incipient hunger to discover deeper meaning and to pursue life differently and more fully. Both Michael and Rachel have provided me with encouragement to believe in the pursuit of life in a more complete and exciting fashion.

I'm a sucker for brilliant storytellers, like rabbis and other teachers who make students work, sweat, and learn. Both Michael and Rachel have these gifts. They're both enchanted by the healing power of life stories.

At the core of the Good Life Seminar, lies the premise that we are learning creatures. We are developed and formed by our diet of learning, step by step, phase by phase. We are what we ingest through our complex learning struggles.

WHAT TO LEARN:

We need to take ourselves seriously—but not too seriously. Character shapers like Michael and Rachel knock us around with their questions, but always with the intent to further our knowledge and to have fun. The very best teachers make us giggle at ourselves, and at our foolish posturing. They can also draw tears, as they tell stories that penetrate our masks.

Readings for Act IV

- *Seasons of Grace* by Alan Jones and John O'Neil—Some rich lessons may be drawn for developing gratitude rituals from this Nautilus Prize-winning book full of stories about how people express gratitude in each season of life.[72]

- *Four Quartets* by T. S. Eliot—In deeply textured language with great intellectual reach, Eliot poses the rich dilemmas of discovering a life worth pursuing. Eliot, like a fine whiskey, must be sipped.[73]

- "Ozymandias" by Percy Bysshe Shelley—This epic ode to a dead king and conqueror features the mighty monuments that time and nature are defacing and eliminating.[74]

POEMS

FOR GOING DEEPER
INTO LIFE

Gratitude Checklist

Got up this morning; checked everything out.
Funny lists we keep,
like a pilot checking out a Dreamliner:
wheels, wings, stuff—check!

Gratitude swells as items are ticked *okay*.
Okay means good to go another trip.
A reason to celebrate, but not to excess.

What about friends and family,
are they checked?
Same ones? Lost ones? New ones?
Check, check, check.
What to do then?
Worry, email, check.

What the hell, let's celebrate our checklists.
How to do that? How is love expressed?
Not with some dreary Browning list.
How do I love you? A flower, a kiss, or
a checklist filled out with gratitude?
Good to go—check!

Organizing Intentions

Recently, in a fit of good intentions,
the boxes got sorted—well, sort of sorted.
Always high purpose triggers these strange fits.

Saving space, ease of use, aesthetics,
Perhaps it's a cheap pledge to live in orderly fashion,
though I'm not sure what order I seek—
is it a higher order?

Does a digger inhabit me, a Leakey with trowels?
Was I after the missing link to my forebears?
Or have I watched some TV crap about found treasures?

Was it granny or a demented uncle
who left me this trove?
Great treasures never actually used, or art unseen?
Could I channel Houdini and make it all vanish?

Now the existential bit—is this death prep?
Should I call an exorcist, a voodooist, a shrink?
Or just rent a storage locker?

And put it all there, with a list.

The Good Life

Once our striving, grasping instincts subside,
we can begin to sketch plans
for abundance, a good life.
We feel tenuous freedom by declaring victory.
We cry out: *What's next?*

Let us continue to tap, tap, tap our daring dance
of not knowing
by sealing off compartments of old ambitions.
We rise, floating on hidden dreams,
enjoying outrageous flirtations with life anew.

Our dusty flutes, songs, flowers can be revived
if we can find them.
By capturing new dreams and outsized hopes,
a good life will kick aside
the chrysalis of habit.

Little by little, dull routines
will find new legs.
Unlikely places will spawn new friends.
They too want a piece of the promised action.

As with Beckett's tramps,
small talk spins into weird
and maybe holy dialogue.
We're all searching for salvation,
but as with other searchers—
Buddha and the prophets—the unexpected happens.
Kinky, fresh, ambitions turn into delicious solutions.
Come. The good life is right here.

Losing Our Labels

Let us be done with confining categories.
Have labels ever truly guided us?
Admiral, goofy, hipster, elder—all tags that destine us
to strut our given roles.

We kill children by affixing sticky names—
skinny, fatty, geek—life sentences all.
To innocent lives, we add burdens.

We must reframe unctuous parents' hopes.
Titles are another name for chains.
Generations must live out X, Y, or Z expectations.

Precious Baby Boomers fought their curse of not knowing
what weird expectations they were supposed to meet.
But they learned to
salsa, jitterbug, and waltz, not just consume.

Be like the diminutive Gandhi telling rude Brits,
"I will not be your old brown-skinned,
starving slave!"

"I'm a thinker." That's my title, my hope
No elder here!

ACT V

BONUS YEARS

[A LA MODE]

··· AGE 80-Who Knows? ···

Michel Eyquem de Montaigne, the great 16th century philosopher and statesman, was one of the most influential writers of the French Renaissance. He's known for popularizing the essay as a literary genre, and particularly for incorporating personal anecdotes into his intellectual insights. Writing about the end of life, he said, "If you don't know how to die, don't worry; Nature will tell you what to do on the spot, fully and adequately. She will do this job perfectly for you; don't bother your head about it."[75] Montaigne lost his father, his best friend, and four children, and came near death himself, while still a relatively young man. Based on his experience, Montaigne advises us to leave death to nature's directions and, instead, learn how to live.

I have had to learn to cope, even grow, from the losses of loved ones that accelerate in frequency in Act V. I have seen many suffer from diminished capacity, being patronized or ignored. Some of us may fret about legacy. I listen to people replay old victories, become sentimental, even maudlin or, like Rabbit in John Updike's book, *Rabbit Redux,*[76] become emotionally frozen by the glory of shooting a high school basketball game's winning shot. To allay natural decay, our banquet tables must be reset with fresh and appealing food, wine, and ideal guests. I definitely needed new guides and savants to help me continue to learn and stoke my curiosity.

Again, Montaigne can be instructive: He liked to organize learning ventures with friends and teachers, often to Italy. He was intrigued by the energy, wisdom, and cultural advances wrought by the Renaissance. So Italy, the center of the Renaissance, was a natural destination. Montaigne would ask for guidance from the Medici family, major sponsors of artists and writers in Florence, during those fecund years. He would arrange a caravan with other enthusiasts, and they would enjoy learning feasts and celebrations on the long trip. Given his propensity to write essays, and the way they were received and distributed all over Europe, he can be said to be a true networker and knowledge disseminator. His essay style influenced Shakespeare, Dickens, and Darwin, who all paid him homage.

Each of us, in our own way, can emulate and honor Montaigne. I have enjoyed the distribution of thoughts and feelings made possible by sharing my own writing, consulting, and learning processes through the Internet. For all its hazards (including a world leader tweeting his biases and threats), the Internet can still be used for learning and caring, and will, no doubt, be increasingly put to new purposes.

Resetting the Act V Table

Fresh culture carriers, character shapers, guides, and sherpas must be found to help us scale this last stretch of the expedition up life's development mountain. Talent and generosity from our own families, new friends and old, teachers, writers, and poets always help. Roles and responsibilities change, often dramatically. Helping friends learn how to face end-of-life experiences is challenging. My job: Be available to serve. Their job: Teach me about courage, and about overcoming fear and pain.

One of these friends goes way back. Bill Swanson, a very tough (former Navy Seal) and highly successful business and family man, called me unexpectedly and asked, "How about meeting for lunch this upcoming weekend?" I said, "Saturday would work," and suggested a place to meet. Bill brought his splendid son, David, and I brought my wife, Pat, who is devoted to Bill.

After being seated, and after beginning with the usual chat about family, politics, books, and theater, Bill said, "I am dying." We kept chatting, so he repeated his words. Then we stopped and asked, "What do you mean?" He then described his medical condition in detail. He reminded me, "Lois and I came to see you in a family crisis once before, and you helped. Now I'm back again seeking that same help." I said, "Of course," and so did Pat. As Pat and I left, we knew we had a whole new challenge ahead of us. On the way home, we discussed how much we loved this man and his family and how honored we felt to be asked to help. Pat, as a wise, well-trained therapist, could provide answers and support that would be invaluable. My role would be much different: I would simply be a trusted, empathetic friend who listens, supports, and learns.

Bill is not the only one with whom I have been honored to have had such sacred, end-of-life sessions. It's part and parcel of engaging in Act V. Very recently, I supported my dear friend and Good Life Seminar co-leader Pete Thigpen, by helping him figure out his exit. Over many months, we met for coffee at Poggio, in Sausalito, to go over the program for our seminars. Then we would shift our talk to Pete's latest test results and the awful discussions one has about late-stage cancer. Finally, about a year ago, Pete said, "I want out of this game. I have had a good run and it's time to cash in." Our conversation then changed to how Pete needed to reset his table going forward. His main criteria was who he could have good conversations with and learn from.

Healthy Communities for Act V

National Geographic Fellow and explorer, Dan Buettner set out in search of hotspots where the world's longest-lived people could be found. Buettner identified five regions as "Blue Zones" (a term he trademarked): Okinawa, Japan; Sardinia, Italy; Nicoya, Costa Rica; Icaria, Greece); and among the Seventh-day Adventists in Loma Linda, California. He began to focus on what these communities, where living to 100 was not out of the ordinary, had in common. He found people who were mindful of eating well, exercising (often gardening and walking), and community caregiving.[77]

If you arrive at 80 in generally good health, with intact family, and a sense of curiosity and humor, you up your odds for having good bonus years. In fact, it may be said that the trifecta of good aging is to arrive at 80 with the following advantages:

- You are still self-propelling, which provides a sense of freedom.

- Your learning is driven by both a keen awareness of where you are in your life, and curiosity.

- Your sense of humor remains intact, and you remember that life is not all about you. Laughter provides our spirits with lubricant, thus protecting them from drying out.

Two of the most beloved wisdom carriers of their time, Mel Brooks and Carl Reiner, were best friends for over 70 years. In the 1950s, they collaborated to create a very funny series of comedy routines in which Brooks plays a 2000-year-old man interviewed by Carl Reiner on the topic of longevity. "The 2000-Year-Old-Man" sketches were recorded on vinyl in the 1960s and later performed on television. Brooks recommends eating fruit (nectarines), getting exercise (outrunning tigers), and meeting famous historical figures (he knew Jesus, personally, and dated Joan of Arc). He mainly extolls the virtues of laughter—not taking ourselves too seriously.[78]

There is no roadmap for navigating the 80s and beyond. I'm grateful to have had experienced guides who thoughtfully shared their journeys with me. John Levy and Joe Henderson were the most helpful in describing their own experiences—the losses and the gains. Both were introverted, so the idea of living with a more inward focus was comfortable for them. I continue to seek and find good company and wise instructors.

General Wisdom

Freedom comes in strange ways, as we move along. There's little need for posturing. Warmth of connection always trumps the need for approbation. Fewer obligations means more room flexibility in charting the course for each day.

- Ambition can be directed toward gaining self-knowledge and developing practices of gratitude for what you possess.

- Dignity is discovered in acts of generosity of spirit. Each gift we offer those in need adds to our stockpile of precious transactions. Giving becomes a way of living fully, quietly, and gently.

- Celebrating small things: people, what shows up, what you forage. Declare early victories and remember: We get to decide what matters and what doesn't. Celebrate that.

The choice is yours about how to live "all in" to the end. A few suggestions might help:

- Focus thoughts and attention on small blessings, precious gifts that you might have rushed by in the past.

- Develop two durable mindsets to live by: gratitude and generosity.

- Shed old grievances, petty quarrels, outrageous fears, and hate lists.

Finding New Guides: Wisdom Carriers and Character Shapers

Steve Edelman

Steve Edelman, a friend who adds wisdom to my life on several aspects of proper living and learning, showed up fairly recently. We share a gracious and generous Pilates teacher. My wife, Pat, met Steve and his wife, Sharon, because of Annie Joseph, a Marin-style couples' yenta. Steve and Sharon had spent their earlier years in the commercial television business. He developed programs; she was an on-air personality; and they co-hosted "Good Morning Minneapolis."

Now in their Act III, the Edelmans are always on the lookout for learning opportunities, and they have found many. For example, they created a video for me to offer as a keynote seminar for top UPS leaders from all over the globe. Steve helped me get the script right, and Sharon interviewed me. It was a fabulous learning experience.

The Edelmans are now in the process of learning how to help aspiring leaders become more effective communicators. Steve and I share an interest in seminars that support people through healthy life changes. His seminar at Esalen is very popular, and he learns alongside the seminarians, as I did with The Good Life Seminar.

W H A T   T O   L E A R N :

At this time in life, I enjoy rituals of good humor with dear friends and family. Act V should be Italian in spirit: every meal an occasion for celebration, small or large. Is it possible to imagine fashioning a Blue Zone in your own community? In an unplanned manner, Pat and I are finding friends and associates with whom to learn, especially regarding fresh ideas, music, poetry, and drama. Sharon and

Steve are healthy members of our informal, sprawling Blue Zone—
Sausalito. My Sausalito Young Men's Book Club is a piece of that Blue
Zone. My poetry class and quiet efforts to write this book are also
learning chips that I play with true joy. Here's a sample:

A Friend Discovered

Who knows where friends come from.
The gym—poetry class—your client?
Googled learning mate and up popped odd topics for courses:
On Tuesday you can sample tantric poker,
Need an earnest, frisky groper?
Sunday the offerings were sparse
Unless you seek a flat-out farce
Of course some pursue friends in bars
Dorothy Parker was one of the bar stars
But she could fashion lines like,
"Wine's fine, but liquor's quicker."
I could only put together,
"What do you think about this weather?"

Paul Sack, Wisdom Carrier

There is something special about a young man who, after achieving a Harvard BA and MBA, chooses to work for the The Emporium, a
small department store chain in San Francisco. His reason? He felt he
needed to understand how a business worked, from the basement up.
Paul Sack would go on to enjoy quiet successes, one after another.

After absorbing what retail could teach him, Paul began to pursue
a new career in real estate, one building at a time. He found his wife,
Prentice, and they started a family, then decided to join the Peace Corps.
They landed in Africa, where a new passion emerged: serving Africans

and finding new members for their family. Paul went on to serve as budget director at Peace Corps headquarters in Washington, D.C., after which the newly constituted family returned to San Francisco.

During all this time, Paul and Prentice expanded their interests including photography, sailing, and opera. Paul's interest in collecting photography ripened into a very special collection of architectural art, part of which resides on the walls of San Francisco's Museum of Modern Art. After Prentice passed, Paul increased his learning ventures and gradually turned the business over to his daughter, Kirby.

Paul continues to learn. After receiving the first-ever PhD in Political Economics granted by UC Berkeley, he created a major real estate REIT with partners and, being a naturally good friend, he kept teaching friends like me, over lovely lunches in his Modern Art-festooned home in San Francisco.

WHAT TO LEARN:

Paul found Shirley, a new learning partner with whom to share his pursuits. The two can be found wherever that opera or art aficionados gather for fresh exploits. Together, they show us that in Act V of life, we must refine our healing story. This involves forgiving those we believe have injured us. We must round out our repertoire of reading, watching, meditating, and learning. We must lean toward the comic, foolish, ironic, and gentle self-deprecation—the healing aspects of life's inflationary drift.

Michel de Montaigne, Wisdom Carrier

Montaigne carried the wisdom of the ages and shared it with us through his compelling writing and his own life story. Montaigne was a 16th century nobleman who owned Chateau d'Yquem, one of the great vineyards and winemaking facilities in the Périgord region of Southwestern France, near Bordeaux. He invented the essay form, and through that device, educated people around the world (and continues to do so). He wrote 107 essays focused on how to live.

Montaigne's interests were wide-ranging. A true autodidact, he traveled to learn. He served as the mayor of Bordeaux, fashioning a great library and study rooms. He turned over the commercial side of his business to others, then focused on reading ancient Greek philosophy, with a bias toward Epicurus and his disciples. But he also read many others including Plutarch, Cicero, Seneca, Pyrrho, and Socrates. His famous take off on Socrates' statement, "All I know is that I know nothing," added, "and I am not even sure about that," which tells us a lot about why Montaigne remained unable to take sides in disputes, especially religious ones. At the time he was actively involved in politics in Bordeaux, the Catholics and Huguenots were in bloody conflict. Although born a Catholic, Montaigne scrupulously avoided taking sides, and that probably saved his life.

Montaigne traveled throughout Europe, especially favoring Italy. On his elaborate trips, he mapped out learning challenges in art, history, and culture, as well as indulging in fine food and wine. He sought out experts to guide his pursuit of knowledge. Perhaps the most important of his explorer-partners was a fellow Bordelais council member and his closest friend, Étienne de La Boétie. Fortunately for scholars like Sarah Bakewell, the exchange of letters between these two friends showed how they learned from each other on a wide range of topics.[79]

WHAT TO LEARN:

Perhaps Montaigne's greatest gift to us was his invention of the essay form and his use of it to address a wide range of disparate topics clustered around the ancient question of how to live. Being an Epicurean, he focused on the use of the senses, and covered a range of topics such as "smells," "how our mind hinders itself," "coaches," and "how we laugh and cry at the same thing."

Because of the huge success of the essay in reaching mass audiences, we have Montaigne to thank for the wild popularity of Charles Dickens's books written as serial newspaper stories. Montaigne's influence is also apparent in the way Charles Darwin broke down his writing into diary stories, and Abraham Lincoln used short, persuasive speeches to win over his audiences. Adam Gopnik writes beautifully about this in his book *Ages and Angels*.[80] We can all view learning and teaching as compressed and interesting short "courses" within the larger feast of life—the good life.

Enchilada as Dessert

After losing my partner of nine years, Pete Thigpen, I wrote a letter putting The Good Life Seminar in mothballs. It was a challenge to write, because I knew the seminarians as friends and co-conspirators. The letter was also a marker, another lovely episode in a magical life.

As I look forward to the next series of life events, such as tossing this book upon the waters, I realize how everything we do can be an addition to life's feast of gratitude. Recently, on a fascinating study trip to Scotland, I found myself looking at dessert menus first. Usually we focus on the entrée and then grudgingly say, "Oh alright, I guess we must at least look at the dessert menu."

One of our dear friends, Emily Marks, had massive cancer surgery that left her digestive system a mess. She could only tolerate soft, mostly white foods. Colorful fruits and high fiber veggies like kale were verboten. One little gift emerged: She could have ice cream and custards. So we found ourselves joining her in looking first to desserts, guilt-free.

Growing up during WWII brought rationing and rearrangement in terms of what and how we ate. We ate what we could get with our government coupons. Sugar was scarce. Our "victory" garden provided fresh peas, spinach, squash, and potatoes, but no dessert. So, on special occasions when we ate out, we checked the desserts first. Who knew that would become another way to celebrate life's banquet, Auntie Mame-style!

It is tempting to add luscious extravagances as the proper way to go through life. However, the old evidence suggests being grateful for what we have, and the new evidence advises avoiding sweets. A hopeful trend in the culinary world is an emphasis on "fresh." For a recent lunch, my brother, Pat, selected Chez Panisse, the celebrated Alice Waters' Berkeley restaurant. I studied the menu, looking at how carefully the food was "sourced." Waters is one of the leaders of the farm-to-table movement, and local sourcing is a big part of her success. Life success is also about mindfully sourcing ideas, learning partners, and guides.

As we consider the five acts of adult life, let's pay special attention to these common elements:

- **Gratitude**—How lucky to have fresh kale and carrots, right?

- **Continuous Learning**—So many things to know, and which to master?

- **Companions**—The company we keep will determine the depth of our experiences and feed our curiosity, the mother's milk of learning.

Readings for Act V

Instructions on how to enjoy Act V can be found in the following resources. These readings may be among the most valuable.

- *Old Age* by Helen Luke—This is a powerful story of the conquering hero, Ulysses, who returns home from his hero's journey only to find that another adventure awaits: the journey inside, to discover who he really is.[81]

- "A Rose for Emily" by William Faulkner—Faulkner uncovers and abiding love in this elegant, wise, and disturbing short story, which many consider his greatest writing.[82]

- *Cut These Words into My Stone* by Michael Wolfe—This collection of ancient epitaphs reveals the broad range of ways in which Greeks of the Golden Age wanted their lives to be remembered.[83]

- *The Best Day the Worst Day* by Donald Hall—A poet's memoir about learning to live alone.[84]

- *Ocean of Wisdom* by the Dalai Lama—Offers wisdom to spare.[85]

- *Rules for Aging: A Wry and Witty Guide to Life* by Roger Rosenblatt—Provides practical advice with plenty of humor.[86]

POEMS
FOR BONUS YEARS

The poems for this stage are about the outrageous challenges inherent in maximizing these precious days. They cover such robust topics as meditation, walking, work, memory, mentors and teachers, and finding one's tribe and heroes. Each one should bring a smile and, I hope, bring to mind someone with whom to share it.

Dancing Trickster

At first, losses of ordinary function seem
to doer and onlooker
like small, anomalous shames.
Then these early failures turn into irritants
that cause spasms of surprising anger.

Then anger inexplicably spins into guilt
too painful to contain,
so we carry it about in a metaphorical sack
and twist again
into insufferable self-pity followed by
lurches of cheap tolerance.

Nothing holds, so we push it all away
with jiving-jittering steps,
all Astaire-like denial
like his puella partners, who
magically stay young.

So we pretend to steps we never mastered,
like dancing on the ceiling.
A neat trick for aging tricksters,
don't you think?

Try it, but don't slip.

Keeping Score

There are many ways to count what matters.
Bankers, accountants, funeral
directors keep dour books.
Brave actuaries know a lot about death.

Priests watch us come and go, come and go.
Time for a new bookkeeping for odd goods,
like laughter, a sweet embrace,
an unexpected smile.

Foot rubs, a child's giggle.
Let the small ones show us how to count bugs
or pet a dog or hold a cat just so.

Ancient ones can fart off-key and laugh.
Lucky savants can find joy in ham and eggs
and other ordinary things.

Or, we can burn our account books.
The hell with aging.
Let's start our devious assaults right now.
You first, with your crossword and baseball scores.

Navigating Adventure Cautiously

Looking down to walk as if land mines wait,
trying to grasp handrails without appearing desperate,
fighting macho pride to accept a helping hand—

the limbs and eyes give us away.
A natural caution can feel like surrender.
Or can we find the guts to rebel
against doubting steps?

Let daring thoughts arise.
Now's the time for a hero's journey.
Imagination and dreams don't need canes.

Madame Curie's derring-do gave us radiation;
Florence Nightingale guided
modern nursing from her bed.
Dare to have unfettered visions of exploration!
Dream of lands explored by Glenn and Shackleton!
But keep the body close to home.

Meditation for Non-Yogis

Learning to meditate is not easy,
but there's no shortage of teaching yogis.
I've tried several;
each had an earnestness that said,
"This is important stuff,
so wake up!"

I was given a swami to help me
teach leaders how to manage anger.
He pitched hard; it seems
he had a school they should attend.
The leaders hated his style;
they grew quite angry, so he left.

A horny yogi said,
"Try tantric meditation!
It will set your chakras all on fire.
You won't find calm and peace,
but your libido will be happy."

In contrast, Thich Nhat Hanh is a lovely man:
very calming—no pitch.
He teaches walking meditation
with peace and love for mantras.
It's a good deal since we all
need to walk more anyway.

The Mind's Filing System

Saw a friend in the aging business—strange work.
Happily, I got his name right,
and his spouse's too.
He has an uncommonly good memory,
handy in his line.

But he's still young, brimming with happy cells.
BTW: Where are our brains cells for compassion?

Can we choose what we remember?
"We can," my friend assured me, but he didn't persuade.
Maybe it's the way we file our memories—like underwear.

If we put the new ones last,
we can grab the oldest first, or is it the
other way around?

A former roommate took a memory course
but forgot where he parked his car.
Wanted his money back, but forgot to ask.
Easy go.

I just recalled an important matter:
It's FIFO we need (first in, first out).
Saves underwear.
Or is it the other way around?

Apps and Chants

Is there a stylish app for salvation?
Got one called Zen Brush;
it comes close.
You can create your own mandala
without the messy sand.

When the monks place the sand
properly, neatly,
how do they also see the gestalt?
Do they have a zoom lens?
Are they gleefully imagining harmony

Another app gets me up and walking.
Writers suffer for their sedentary ways.
It scolds: "Move your limbs!"
It nags!

The Dalai Lama says he dies every day for practice.
It makes him laugh.
Me too, for him.
Are our apps too bloody serious?

I like to think Steve Jobs is writing
an app for reincarnation.
Let's squat and celebrate our next iPhone app that chants
a start toward salvation.
Om—go!

An Ode to John Gardner

"What have you learned since
we last met?"
His greetings inspired, his
smile warmed.
Tall and uncommonly handsome, John
was a keen student, a beloved teacher.

We first met when I was a rookie
at AT&T.
I heard him talk about leadership
and I followed.
John thought good leaders deserved
good followers.

As the years went by, he collected
many trophies
for leadership and writing.
As Secretary of Health, Education and Welfare
under Lyndon Johnson,
he quietly guided the Civil Rights Movement,
gave LBJ cover from Republicans.

His reputation rose;
Washington and the world took note,
and then he left.

One day he called and asked
what I thought.
"Should I return to Stanford and teach?"
I said of course, selfishly, because
I needed his teaching and company.

With a firm hand he guided
many of us.
He celebrated our small-beer
achievements
and always asked, "And what
have you learned since we last met?"

Gordon Sherman, a Proper Prophet

One Sunday, my friend Gordie
called, surprisingly.
In his deep, cultivated CEO voice,
he announced his coming!
A resident of Chicago, he was
to be my new neighbor.

It seems some callous doctors had
given him months
to live. He had cancer.
But his answer to their dreaded prognosis
was to fire them!

"I will be your new neighbor,
and we'll have fun,"
he continued,
as I struggled to gain composure.
"Of course," I replied.
"We'll go fishing."

He found new doctors, who inspired.
On a sacred stream, he taught me
fishing and opera.
He cooked and sang arias
from memory.

Each month after "the tests,"
we would rejoice.
With red wine and good Italian food,
we celebrated one more month.
He taught me for a dozen glorious years.

"Dying is a wonderful way to live
if it doesn't kill you," he laughed.
I still remember his wit and will.
And I try to apply his teaching
every grateful day:
eat fish and Italian.

An Almost-New Song

They come unhidden, ancient tunes long gone.
What causes the humming—
has a circuit clicked open?
A few words arrive with a sweet bit of beat—

"Fly me to the moon" might just show up.
Hum me!
Or a few bars of a love song once poignant
then put away carelessly.

Now to the words, those cool Sinatra phrases.
A few lines feel right, but then they disappear.
Next the fake crap, *la de da* and a bit more—
like watching lip-synched drunks karaoke.
You know, all soulful, passionate, real James Brown.
Who was your dance partner for this bit?
Cool, but horny—do you recall?

The words are gone, like Alice down the rabbit hole.
They hide like unicorns with their magical horn.
Please come when I call.
Let's sing—okay?

AFTERWORD
A CALL TO ACTION

...

Writing Your Own Gratitude Memoir

I intended this book to not only be a guide for living the good life, but also an invitation to write your own gratitude memoir as a healing legacy. The framework I chose focuses on what I have learned in each act of life development. It honors those who taught me—the influential teachers and guides who arrived in my life at just the right time.

An unanticipated joy has been blossoming, as many friends who read parts of this book-in-progress have grown excited about and gained traction in writing their own gratitude memoirs. Now I urge you, too, to consider capturing your accumulated experiences and wisdom as a legacy.

Exploring the Healing Framework

As an avid student of C.G. Jung, I discovered that one of his acolytes, James Hillman, wrote a splendidly wise book called *Healing Fiction*. In this profound work, Hillman asks, "If we are telling a fictionalized version of our life story (and we are), why not invent a healing one?"[87] *Life: The Whole Enchilada* is a testament to Hillman's idea. I love his core proposition because it feels right and actually works. I know because I tried it and it delivers.

To write this form of healing memoir, your task is to describe what you learned in each act of adult development, and to describe the actors who helped you (not necessarily in that order). The method is to answer the following questions:

- What can I pass along to others about what I've learned so far?

- Who showed up to teach and guide me along the way? (Recount the circumstances.)

- Can I recollect other sources of wisdom that were helpful and may serve to stir readers?

- How can I be more generous in sharing credits? (Remember: Gratitude is what heals us.)

WHAT TO LEARN

In the martial art of Aikido, students are urged to "steal" their teacher's technique, and down the road, by layering on their own experiences, they will eventually make the technique their own. I welcome you to steal my framework and make it your own!

For more information about the ideas in this book and how to write your own gratitude memoir, please visit:

www.redpeppermoon.com

Acknowledgements

So many friends' contributions made this book possible.
Some are mentioned, but many are not. My children and grandchildren,
who play many roles in my life, have been tolerant listeners to my latest
ravings, and kind, empathetic voices who guide me back when I am lost.

A special shout out to Grace Vannelli, a dear friend, granddaughter
and talented artist who designed the cover of this book and generally
kept the production process going. I am also grateful to my son-in-law,
Todd Whitaker, for his organizing advice and general support, as well as
to Kathryn Klein for providing welcome, fresh eyes and whose
elegant editing helped make sense of the whole book.

Endnotes

1. John R. O'Neil, *The Paradox of Success: When Winning at Work Means Losing at Life* (G.P. Putnam's Sons, 1994)

2. Alan Jones and John R. O'Neil, *Seasons of Grace: The Life-Giving Practice of Gratitude* (John Wiley & Sons, 2003)

3. William James, "A Plea for Psychology as a Natural Science" (1892), *Collected Essays and Reviews* (1920)

4. Virginia Woolf, "The Leaning Tower" (lecture delivered to the Workers' Educational Association, Brighton, May 1940), *The Moment and Other Essays* (1948)

5. William Shakespeare, *As You Like It* (1599 or 1600)

6. H.L. Mencken, "The Divine Afflatus" in *New York Evening Mail* (16 November 1917); later published in *Prejudices: Second Series* (Jonathan Cape, 1920) and *A Mencken Chrestomathy* (Random House, 1949)

7. Michel de Montaigne, *Essais* (written between 1571 and 1592, first published in various editions between 1580 and 1595, full text of Charles Cotton translation online at the Gutenberg Project), Book I, Ch. 31 ("...il n'est rien creu si fermement que ce qu'on sçait le moins,")

8. H.G. Wells, *The Outline of History* (1920), Ch. 41

9. Abraham Maslow, *Motivation and Personality* (Harpers, 1954)

10. Jerome Lawrence and Robert Edwin Lee, *Auntie Mame* (Broadway play, 1956), based on the novel by Patrick Dennis (1955), later adapted for a film directed by Morton DaCosta (1958), and not to be confused the Broadway musical version (1966), music and lyrics by Jerry Herman, that was later adapted by Paul Zindel for the film, *Mame*, directed by Gene Saks. The line, "Life is a banquet and most poor suckers are starving to death," does not appear in the original novel. In the 1956 stage play, it was originally, "Life is a banquet and most poor sons-of-bitches are starving to death." Although "damn" and "hell" are both heard in the 1958 film version, "sons-of-bitches" was apparently thought too rough and was changed to "suckers."

11. Joseph Campbell, *The Hero with a Thousand Faces* (1st ed., Pantheon Press, 1949); revised by Campbell (2nd ed., Princeton University Press, 1968)

12. Homer, *The Odyssey* <http://www.gutenberg.org/ebooks/1728>

13. Harper Lee, *To Kill a Mockingbird* (1st ed., J.B. Lippincott & Co., 1960)

14. Arnold Toynbee, *Civilization on Trial* (Oxford University Press, 1948)

15. J.D. Salinger, *The Catcher in the Rye* (1st ed. Little, Brown and Company, 1951)

16. Jerry Leiber and Mike Stoller, "Is That All There Is," (lyrics © Sony/ATV Music Publishing LLC, Warner Chappell Music, Inc., 1968)

17. Marcus Aurelius, *Meditations, Book 12*, paragraph 1 (ca. 170-180 C.E.) A more verbose but perhaps more accurate translation: "If then, whatever the time may be when thou shalt be near to thy departure, neglecting everything else thou shalt respect only thy ruling faculty and the divinity within thee, and if thou shalt be afraid not because thou must some time cease to live, but if thou shalt fear never to have begun to live according to nature – then thou wilt be a man worthy of the universe which has produced thee, and thou wilt cease to be a stranger in thy native land, and to wonder at things which happen daily as if they were something unexpected, and to be dependent on this or that."

18. <https://quoteinvestigator.com/2012/12/18/age-mind/>

19. Bill Bridges, *Transitions: Making the Most of Change* (Da Capo Lifelong Books, 2004)

20. Gail Sheehy, *Passages: Predictable Crises of Adult Life* (Dutton, 1976)

21. Jonas Salk, *Survival of the Wisest* (Harper & Row, 1973)

22. Homer, *The Iliad* <http://www.gutenberg.org/ebooks/6130> and The Odyssey <http://www.gutenberg.org/ebooks/1728>

23. Lewis Carroll, *Alice's Adventures in Wonderland* (1st ed. 1871), Chapter II, "'Curiouser and curiouser!' cried Alice (she was so much surprised, that for the moment she quite forgot how to speak good English); `now I'm opening out like the largest telescope that ever was! Good-bye, feet!' (for when she looked down at her feet, they seemed to be almost out of sight, they were getting so far off). `Oh, my poor little feet, I wonder who will put on your shoes and stockings for you now, dears? I'm sure I shan't be able!'"

24. T.H. White, *The Once and Future King* (Collins, 1958), Chapter 21

25. John Gardner, *Self-Renewal: The Individual and the Innovative Society* (1st ed., Harper & Row, 1963)

26. Thomas Kuhn, *The Structure of Scientific Revolutions* (1st ed., University of Chicago Press, 1962)

27. Salk, *Survival of the Wisest*, op. cit.

28. Edna St. Vincent Millay, "Figs from Thistles: First Fig," first published in *Poetry: A Magazine of Verse*, Edited by Harriet Monroe, Volume 11, Number 3, June 1918 (Chicago, Illinois, 1918), p. 130

29. Salinger, *The Catcher in the Rye*, op.cit.

30. White, *The Once and Future King*, op. cit.

31. John Steinbeck, *The Works of King Arthur and His Noble Knights* (Farrar, Straus & Giroux, 1976

32. Homer, *The Iliad,* op. cit.

33. Salinger, *The Catcher in the Rye*, op. cit.

34. Hermann Hesse, *Siddhartha* (first published in 1920, 1st American ed., New Directions, 1951)

35. Miguel de Cervantes, *The Ingenious Gentleman Don Quixote of La Mancha* (first published in two parts, in 1605 and 1615)

36. Mihaly Csikszentmihalyi, *Flow: The Psychology of Optimal Experience* (1st ed., Harper & Row, 1990)

37. Michael Jordan, "60 Minutes" interview with Ed Bradley (CBS News, 2005)

38. Muhammad Ali (known by his birth name Cassius Clay, Jr. at the time of the quote), just before entering the ring to fight Sonny Liston in Miami Beach, Florida in 1964

39. Michael Jordan, as quoted in *Nike Culture: The Sign of the Swoosh*, by Robert Goldman and Stephen Papson, (Sage Publications, 1998), 49

40. Barbara Bradley Hagerty, *Life Reimagined: The Science, Art, and Opportunity of Midlife* (Penguin Publishing Group, 2016)

41. David Brooks, "The Middle-Age Surge," *The New York Times* (March 22, 2016)

42. John Gardner, *Self-Renewal*, op. cit.

43. Brooks, "The Middle-Age Surge," op. cit.

44. Gareth Hill, *The Shaman from Elko*, (Sigo Press, 1978)

45. Walt Whitman, "Song of Myself," *Leaves of Grass* (1st ed. self-published,1855)

46. White, *The Once and Future King*, op. cit.

47. Sarah Bakewell, *How to Live: Or A Life of Montaigne in One Question and Twenty Attempts at an Answer* (UK: Chatto & Windus, 2010; US: Other Press, 2011)

48. F. Scott Fitzgerald, *The Great Gatsby* (US: Charles Scribner's Sons, 1925; UK: Chatto & Windus, 1926)

49. Betty Friedan, *The Feminine Mystique* (W. W. Norton, 1963)

50. George Leonard, *Mastery: The Keys to Success and Long-Term Fulfillment* (1st ed. Dutton Books, 1991)

51. John R. O'Neil, *Leadership Aikido* (Harmony, 1997)

52. Dalai Lama XIV, *How to Practice* (Pocket Books, 2002)

53. Ann Morrow Lindberg, *Gifts from the Sea* (Pantheon Books, 1955)

54. O'Neil, *The Paradox of Success*, op. cit.

55. Oliver Sacks, *Musicophilia: Tales of Music and the Brain* (Knopf, 2007)

56. Dylan Thomas, "Do not go gentle into that good night," *The Poems of Dylan Thomas* (New Directions, 1952)

57. Gardner, *Self-Renewal*, op. cit.

58. Bridges, *Transitions*, op. cit.

59. Winston S. Churchill, *Painting as a Pastime* (Whittlesey House McGraw-Hill Book Company, Inc, 1950)

60. Anthony Storr, *Churchill's Black Dog, Kafka's Mice, and Other Phenomena of the Human Mind* (Grove Press, 1989)

61. Betty Edwards, *Drawing on the Right Side of the Brain* (first published in 1979; 4th definitive, deluxe, expanded, updated ed., TarcherPerigee, 2012)

62. Roger Rosenblatt, *Rules for Aging: A Wry and Witty Guide to Life* (Harvest, 2001)

63. Mark Chimsky (ed.), *80 Things to Do When You Turn 80* (Sellers Publishing, Inc., 2017)

64. Churchill, *Painting as a Pastime*, op. cit.

65. Ricardo B. Levy, *Letters to a Young Entrepreneur: Succeeding in Business Without Losing at Life* (first published in 2010; 2nd definitive, expanded, updated ed., 2015)

66. Helen Luke, *Old Age: Journey into Simplicity* (Parabola Books, 1987)

67. Marcus Tullius Cicero, *Oratio Pro Cnæo Plancio, XXXII* (c. 63 CE). Note that there is some dispute about the correct translation of this quote, and many substitute "mother" for "parent." Here are two viewpoints: 1) "A current University of Chicago translation more accurately includes an original meaning lost in many later translations, that of not merely feeling grateful, but also of showing gratitude: '...the being and appearing grateful. For this one virtue is not only the greatest, but is also the parent of all the other virtues.'—<https://en.wikiquote.org/wiki/Talk:Cicero#Gratitude>; 2) "A thankful heart is not only the greatest virtue but the parent of all the other virtues."—Jehiel Keeler Hoyt, *Hoyt's New Cyclopedia of Practical Quotations* (Funk & Wagnalls Company, 1922), 336-37

68. Thich Nhat Hanh, "Thich Nhat Hanh on Walking Meditation," *The Lion's Roar: Buddhist Wisdom for Our Time* (May 31, 2019) < https://www.lionsroar.com/how-to-meditate-thich-nhat-hanh-on-walking-meditation/>

69. Michael Wolfe, *Cut These Words into My Stone: Ancient Greek Epitaphs* (Johns Hopkins University Press, 2013)

70. William Faulkner, speech at the Nobel Banquet at the City Hall in Stockholm, December 10, 1950 for the Nobel Prize in Literature <https://www.nobelprize.org/prizes/literature/1949/faulkner/speech/>

71. Rachel Naomi Remen, *Kitchen Table Wisdom: Stories that Heal* (10th Anniversary Edition, Riverhead Books, 2006)

72. Jones and O'Neil, *Seasons of Grace*, op. cit.

73. T. S. Eliot, *Four Quartets* (1st ed. US: Harcourt, 1941)

74. Percy Bysshe Shelley, "Ozymandias" (first published in the *The Examiner of London*, January 11, 1818); <https://www.poetryfoundation.org/poems/46565/ozymandias>

75. Michel de Montaigne, attributed (16th c.) <https://en.wikiquote.org/wiki/Michel_de_Montaigne#Attributed>

76. John Updike, *Rabbit Redux* (Alfred A. Knopf, 1971)

77. Dan Buettner, *The Blue Zones: Lessons for Living Longer from the People Who've Lived the Longest* (2nd ed., National Geographic, 2012)

78. Mel Brooks and Carl Reiner, *The 2000 Year Old Man* (originally recorded, Pickwick 33/Capitol Records, 1960; *The Complete 2000 Year Old Man* (box set, audio CD, Rhino, 1994)

79. Bakewell, *How to Live*, op. cit.

80. Adam Gopnik, *Angels and Ages*, (Vintage Books, 2010)

81. Luke, *Old Age*, op. cit.

82. William Faulkner, "A Rose for Emily," (first published in *The Forum*, 1930), *Collected Stories of William Faulkner* (Random House, 1950)

83. Wolfe, *Cut These Words into My Stone*, op. cit.

84. Donald Hall, *The Best Day the Worst Day: Life with Jane Kenyon* (Houghton Mifflin Harcourt, 2005)

85. Dalai Lama XIV, *Ocean of Wisdom: Guidelines for Living* (Clear Light Publishers, 1989)

86. Rosenblatt, *Rules for Aging*, op. cit.

87. James Hillman, *Healing Fiction* (Station Hill Press, 1983)